LONG ISLAND'S
ISLAND'S
Vanished
H E I R E S S

LONG ISLAND'S
Vanished
HEIRESS

THE UNSOLVED
ALICE PARSONS KIDNAPPING

STEVEN C. DRIELAK

THE
History
PRESS

Published by The History Press
Charleston, SC
www.historypress.com

Copyright © 2020 by Steven C. Drielak
All rights reserved

First published 2020

Manufactured in the United States

ISBN 9781467146791

Library of Congress Control Number: 2020932079

There are only three possible theories in this case:
The Kidnap Theory;
The Voluntary Disappearance Theory;
The Murder Theory

—Inspector Earl J. Connelley, FBI

CONTENTS

Preface   11
Acknowledgements   13

1. The Kidnapping   15
2. Alice McDonell Parsons   23
3. William H. Parsons Jr.   35
4. Anna Kupryanova   39
5. The Investigation Begins   47
6. The FBI Takes Over   61
7. War among the Investigators   73
8. The Search   85
9. The Lies   97
10. Letters from the Kidnappers   129
11. The Connelley Gambit   145
12. Leaving Town   149
13. The California Debacle   157

Epilogue   191
Bibliography   197
About the Author   205

PREFACE

The 1930s were a tumultuous time in our nation's history. As the country emerged from the Prohibition era, Americans found themselves facing a new kind of criminal and a new kind of crime. As the 1930s began, the country was captivated by the misdeeds of headline-grabbing criminals like John Dillinger, Baby Face Nelson, Pretty Boy Floyd, Machine Gun Kelly, Ma Barker and Bonnie and Clyde. In addition to breeding a whole new generation of notorious killers, the 1930s also bred a new type of crime: the kidnapping. Abduction for ransom became one of the big-money crimes, along with prostitution, alcohol and drug trafficking. From 1930 to 1932 more than two thousand individuals were abducted for ransom in this country. These events were capped by the kidnapping and murder of twenty-month-old Charles Lindbergh Jr. from his home in East Amwell, New Jersey, in 1932.

Our nation's response to these heinous crimes was twofold. First, Congress passed new legislation in the form of the "Lindbergh Law," which made kidnapping a federal crime if the victim was taken across state lines. The law also allowed for federal jurisdiction whenever a ransom note was placed into the U.S. mail system. Secondly, the U.S. government began to consolidate its federal investigative resources into one large and highly effective organization. That consolidation led to the 1935 creation of the Federal Bureau of Investigation (FBI), which would be led by John Edgar Hoover for the next thirty-seven years.

The story of the alleged kidnapping that took place on the morning of June 9, 1937, at the Long Meadow Farm on Long Island has, until now, been told only by its three main witnesses. These witnesses told a story that caught the attention of an entire nation and led to one of the most expansive investigations in the FBI's then-short history. The news of the kidnapping of heiress Alice McDonell Parsons from her twenty-two-acre farm was splashed across the front page of every major newspaper in the country. This criminal act would eventually pit the mind of one of the FBI's most talented and experienced inspectors against the mind of a simple Russian housekeeper. In the end, only one would win this battle of wills, and in the end, one did.

Acknowledgements

My special thanks to the Three Village Historical Society's archivist Karen Martin for all of her encouragement and assistance.

1

The Kidnapping

June 9, 1937

At 6:30 a.m. on the morning of June 9, 1937, the four occupants of a modest farmhouse located in Stony Brook, New York, began their day. William H. Parsons Jr., the owner of Long Meadow Farm, started his morning by putting his trousers on over his pajamas and a sweater over his shirt before leaving the house to feed the pigeons and other poultry livestock on his twenty-two-acre farm. On his walk back to the house, he stopped into the farm's detached garage, which housed the family car. The car was a new tan-colored Dodge sedan with chromium trim that he had purchased just three months before from the Newcomb Brothers in the nearby village of Port Jefferson. He slipped into the driver's seat, turned over the engine and pulled the car up to the rear of the house. Going back into the house, he proceeded directly to his upstairs bedroom and changed into business attire for his upcoming journey into New York City. Once dressed, William joined his wife, Alice; their Russian housekeeper, Anna Kupryanova; and the housekeeper's ten-year-old son, Roy, at the breakfast table.

There was nothing special about that morning's breakfast table conversation. William and Alice spoke about the maintenance that needed to be done on a piece of property known as the "Sammis place," which Alice had recently inherited from her uncle Colonel Timothy Williams. The property was part of a large estate called Shoreland in the town of Huntington. They also talked about a house painter by the name of Frederick Hubbs whom they were considering hiring to paint the kitchen and butler's pantry at the Sammis place. Alice reminded William that she would be traveling to Huntington that day and would leave a note for Hubbs in his mailbox regarding the color scheme requested by the new tenant of the Sammis place.

The property was about to be rented to Ruth Burdin. The agreement to rent the property to her had just been reached, and the only people aware of the agreement were Burdin, William and Alice.

At the conclusion of breakfast and out of the earshot of young Roy, William and Alice had a discussion regarding the purchases William was to make while he was in New York City that day. One of these purchases included a quiver of arrows for Roy's upcoming eleventh birthday, which was just three days away.

The vast majority of William Parsons's days were spent working on the farm. This business trip to New York City had been hastily arranged the day before and was known only to him, Alice, Anna and those he was to meet in New York City.

At the time, the Parsonses and their housekeeper ran a small business from Long Meadow Farm. They raised squabs and sold canned squab and squab paste to various high-end grocers throughout the area. The original recipe for the squab paste had been provided by housekeeper Anna, which made her a key operator within the small family business. Unfortunately, they had seen little profit from this business venture and considered dropping the enterprise.

In the fall of 1936, the three of them jointly settled on one final effort to increase sales. They had thought at first to arrange with Macy's department store in New York City to make a display of their canned squab but abandoned the idea due to the low market price for squab at that time. They felt that there was more of a market for the squab paste than there was for the canned squabs. With this in mind, Anna Kupryanova took the next step to increase profitability when she wrote to her longtime friend and Russian contact Kyra Malkovsky to arrange the meeting in New York City that day between William Parsons and Baron George Tuve of the Macoroff Company. The Macoroff Company was a major distributor of Russian caviar. Anna and the Parsonses believed that the Macaroff Company could advise them on how to best make their squab paste business profitable.

At 7:35 that morning, Mr. and Mrs. Parsons got into their new Dodge sedan, with William driving, and headed for the St. James train station just a short distance from the farm. The temperature outside was a moderate 65 degrees with a light overcast sky. Local showers were expected all during that day and evening. The drive to the St. James train station took them only ten minutes. Upon arrival at the train station, William parked his car at the curb opposite the local stationery store, at a point opposite where the end of the train usually stopped. William entered the station building to purchase his train ticket. He then went into the stationery store, where he noticed two or three strange men who had the disheveled appearance of individuals who had been up all night. The man behind the counter had the same appearance. William purchased a copy of the *New York Times* and returned to his car. He and Alice talked in the car until the Long Island Rail Road train arrived a few minutes later.

During this brief conversation, William reminded Alice that she was to pick him up at the Huntington train station that evening. Alice, as they had discussed at breakfast, was planning to be in the Huntington area that day, and William enjoyed the evening car ride from Huntington to Stony Brook. When the 7:46 a.m. train for New York City arrived, William got out of the car and said goodbye to Alice as she slid behind the steering wheel. As William boarded the train, Alice steered the Dodge for home. It was the last time that they would ever see each other.

While William and Alice were at the train station, their housekeeper, Anna Kupryanova, busied herself in the kitchen, washing the breakfast dishes and preparing Roy's lunch for school. It was approximately 8:00 a.m. when Alice waved to Roy as she passed him riding his bicycle on his way to school. He was only two hundred feet from the farm's driveway when they passed each other.

Roy had left for school on his bicycle a little earlier than usual that day because he was to stop by Mrs. Melville's Tea House in Stony Brook and water some of her plants. Once he arrived at the Tea House, he saw that it was still closed, so he continued on to his school, where he met two of his friends, Albert Jewell and Clarence Kenney. He stayed with his friends for a while and then returned to the Tea House to complete his chores before school started that morning.

On her return to the farm, Alice parked the Dodge at a slight angle at the rear of the house. Inside, she and Anna talked about the flowers that were to be taken to the flower exchange at the Three Village Garden Club in Stony Brook. They also spoke about an inspection of the pigeons that had not been done the day before, due to other business in Huntington. Alice, as was her custom, dried the breakfast dishes, made the two beds in her and William's room, dusted and laundered some of her personal clothing.

Knowing the exact time of day at Long Meadow Farm could be challenging at times. It seems that Anna's clock in the kitchen was always running thirty minutes fast or thirty minutes slow. All of the members of the household made fun of her clock and referred to it as "Russian Time."

Alice proceeded to check the pigeons, making written notations on the cards attached to the nests; these indicated the age of the eggs or the squabs. As Alice worked with the pigeons, Anna fixed guineas in the chicken yard and took an injured gosling to the farmhouse to have its leg bandaged. Alice joined her there, and together they worked on the gosling's leg.

While Alice and Anna were in the kitchen working on the injured gosling, the Cox garbage truck drove up the driveway and stopped at the back door of the farmhouse. There were two men on the truck: Arthur Chadwick and George Winfield. Arthur got off the truck to collect the Parsons garbage. Most of the garbage was kept in a big can located outside, at the back of the house, next to the bayberry bushes. The garbage was always set outside, and none of the garbage men ever had to go into the basement for garbage. Several squabs had been killed in the basement the day before, resulting in a large box of feathers that needed to go onto the truck. Anna went to the basement and retrieved the box of feathers and, with Alice holding open the inward-swinging kitchen door, set the box of feathers down outside for the garbage men to remove. Without a word being spoken by anyone, Arthur Chadwick picked up the box of feathers and threw it onto the truck.

After the garbage men left, Anna returned to the kitchen and sat in a chair by the table, holding the injured gosling in her lap while Alice applied an adhesive bandage to its leg. At about 11:00 a.m. (approximately five minutes after the garbage men left), an automobile could be heard coming to a grinding halt in the driveway.

A two-door black sedan bearing a New York license plate had stopped about fifteen feet from the back door of the house. The front of the car directly faced the rear porch. Anna had a clear view from her kitchen chair and could clearly see into the front seat of the sedan. She observed a woman sitting on the passenger side of the front seat. She appeared to be approximately forty-five years old and had a round, full face, thick jowls and heavy shoulders and an unusually large bust. She was dressed in a plain blue dress and wore a blue straw hat with a low crown. A middle-aged man sat behind the steering wheel of the sedan. His face was longer than the woman's, and he had a sallow complexion. He was wearing a dark felt hat and a gray suit. Neither the man nor the woman appeared to notice that they were being observed by Alice and Anna from the farmhouse's kitchen. Alice rose from the table and exited the house through the office door. As Alice approached the passenger door of the visitors' sedan, she was joined by Smoky, one of her wire-haired terriers.

As Alice was approaching the couple in the black sedan, William was busy attending to his business in New York City. On his arrival at Pennsylvania

Station, he stopped for a shoeshine in the terminal. He then proceeded to the Rogers Peet Clothing store at 36th Street and Broadway and purchased a new belt. He put the purchase on his charge account. From there, he went to Macy's, where he purchased moth repellent, a pair of shoes and a quiver of arrows for young Roy. During this morning shopping spree, he also visited Brooks Brothers on Madison Avenue and eventually ended up ordering a pair of trousers at F.R. Tripler & Company, just a block away from Brooks Brothers. As his 11:30 a.m. meeting time approached, he began his walk toward the Grand Central Palace located between 46th and 47th Streets. This six-story exhibition hall contained the offices of the Macoroff Company.

As Anna continued her work in the kitchen, Alice conversed with the visitors. Although Anna could not hear what was being said, she did hear Alice laugh at some point in the conversation. A few minutes later, Anna left the kitchen through the dining room, leaving the injured gosling wrapped in an old pair of knickers in the kitchen. As she stepped through the office door to the yard, she noticed both the man and woman glance her way. She then headed for the brooder house, which was some distance from the main farmhouse. Once there, she lost sight of both Alice and the visitors.

Anna remained in the brooder house just long enough to hold and feed six goslings "by the beak." Just as Anna was finishing this task, Alice entered the brooder house. It was obvious that Alice had changed from her earlier clothes and was now wearing a blue ensemble, which consisted of a blue skirt and blue polka-dotted blouse, a dark blue low-crowned felt hat turned up on the left side, rose-beige silk stockings and brown shoes.

Alice stated that she was going to the Sammis place and that there was an old lady interested in the place who could not get there. Anna was somewhat confused by this statement and had decided that Alice had really meant that the old lady could not come to the Parsons farm. Alice then told Anna that she would pick up a pot roast for dinner while she was in Huntington and that she would return later for lunch. Alice then left Anna and headed for the visitors' waiting car. Anna followed a minute later with several goslings held in her pulled-up skirt. As she reached the rear of the garage, she saw the black sedan just as it reached the end of the driveway and turned south onto the main road. Anna noted that the man was driving and that both Alice and the woman visitor were now in the back seat. She also noted that Alice was sitting directly behind the driver.

Anna brought her goslings to a crate next to the cherry tree and retrieved a trowel from the garden house. She proceeded to cultivate the flower garden, which was located next to the dog kennel. While Anna was working in the garden, the phone bell rang in the garage. It was Mr. Ketchum, the stationmaster at the Stony Brook train station. He told Anna that Mr. Parsons had ordered a special wagon for the farm and that it had arrived that morning. A second call came in a short time later. This one was from Mr. Elderkin, the local butcher in St. James, who wanted to know if the Parsons had any squabs to sell.

As Anna was working in the garden, William was meeting with Mr. Rozaroff and Baron Touve of the Macoroff Company. During the hour-long meeting, Baron Touve and William discussed the difficulties William was having marketing his squab paste. Touve recommended that William retain a large distributor such as R.C. Williams & Company for his product and provided William with a contact at the company by the name of Mr. Diflo.

At the conclusion of the meeting, William headed for the Chanin Building at Lexington and 42nd Street, where he ordered lunch at Longchamps Restaurant. After lunch, he left the restaurant and again stopped into Tripler's clothing store and asked them to hold the trousers he had ordered until the following week, when he expected to be in town again to try them on. He then took the 7th Avenue subway downtown to the Christopher Street station and called on the printing firm of Porter and Brooks located on Hudson Street to discuss the creation of a display carton to be used for shipping the squab paste.

William met with Norman Porter and arranged to have a price quote for printed boxes mailed to him. He wanted to know the cost of this type of item before he spoke with anyone from the R.C. Williams distribution company. At some point between 3:00 and 3:30 p.m., William telephoned Tripler & Company and canceled his order for the new pair of trousers. This was followed by a stop at the Biltmore Hotel in order to make a telephone call to Mr. Diflo at the R.C. Williams Company, and a return trip to Macy's to get a second look at a hammock he was interested in. His last stop was the Pennsylvania Hotel, where he enjoyed a couple of glasses of beer before his train ride home. He then left the hotel, crossed over 7th Avenue and entered Pennsylvania Station. Once inside, he checked the train board and headed for the 4:37 p.m. train to Huntington.

Anna's afternoon was a busy one. It began with her lunch of cheese, toast and milk. She then washed some of her undergarments and placed them on the fenders of the Parsonses' car to dry. It was at about this time that the delivery man for the Chemical Carbon Company arrived to deliver a cylinder of gas. Once the clothes were hung to dry and the gas cylinder delivery complete, Anna made several trips to the chicken yard, repaired one of her dresses on the sewing machine and cooked some French-fried onions she intended to take to the Village Tea House the next day.

As Anna was cooking the onions, she heard another vehicle enter the driveway. Anna went to the door and saw Anita Gumbus, whose husband ran a machine shop in Stony Brook, pulling her car up to the house. Alice Parsons had visited Mrs. Gumbus at her home the previous week and asked if she would wash the windows of the Three Village Tea House. Mrs. Gumbus had washed the windows and was now at the Parsons farm in order to collect her payment for the work. With Anita Gumbus were her friends Esther Hawkins and Vera Fallon. When Anita got out of her car and approached the house, Anna appeared at the door. Anna advised Mrs. Gumbus that Mrs. Parsons was in Huntington that afternoon. Mrs. Gumbus thanked her and promptly left the farm.

Once school was let out that afternoon, Roy met with his friend Harold Kerwin for a short time and then went to see his friend Johnny Boshinski, and together they hunted for birds' nests. When he arrived home at approximately 5:30 p.m., he asked his mother for a peppermint candy. She told him he would have to earn it.

William stepped off the train at the Huntington Station at 5:45 p.m. He checked the predesignated meeting spot on New York Avenue that he and Alice had agreed on that morning. Alice was not there. When she did not appear by 6:00 p.m., William walked to a nearby stationery store and telephoned the farm in Stony Brook.

Anna answered the telephone. William asked Anna if she knew where Alice was, and Anna told him that Alice had left at 11:30 that morning with a man and a woman to see the Sammis house and had not yet returned. Anna advised William to take a taxi home.

He then left the stationery store and returned to the designated meeting spot. He waited another few minutes and then decided to call George Taylor, the groundskeeper at the Shoreland Estate. He did not reach Mr. Taylor, but talked to his son, Jimmy. Jimmy stated that he did not think that Mrs. Parsons had been there that day but that his father would be available in about fifteen minutes. William told Jimmy that he would call back shortly and would be asking his father for a ride back to the farm in Stony Brook.

After William hung up the telephone, he suddenly recalled that there was another eastbound train due shortly that would take him to the St. James Station. This train was due to arrive in Huntington at 6:17 p.m. This particular train was running late that evening and William did not arrive at the St. James Station until 7:00 p.m. Once at the station, William went directly to the taxi stand. There he spoke with taxi driver John Masterson and inquired how much the fare would be to his home in Stony Brook. Masterson charged him seventy-five cents.

Upon reaching the farm, Masterson swung into the circular driveway behind the Parsonses' home. As Masterson was pulling up to the back entrance, Anna Kupryanova came out of the back door. As William was getting of the taxi, Anna asked, "Isn't she with you?"

As the taxi pulled away, William and Anna entered the house through the back door. The time now was approximately 7:30 p.m.

Once inside the house, William asked Anna to repeat her story about the two people with whom Alice had left that morning. William then made two telephone calls. The first call was to George Taylor at Shoreland. Taylor told him that he had not seen Mrs. Parsons that day, but he would go down to the Sammis place and check for her. His second call was to Ruth Burdin, who had recently agreed to rent the Sammis place. William was aware of the fact that Mrs. Burdin had an elderly mother, and from what Anna had said regarding an elderly woman not being able to visit in person, he believed that Mrs. Burdin may have had some information regarding Alice's whereabouts. William managed to reach Mrs. Burdin by telephone, and she advised him that she had been in New York City all day and had not seen Mrs. Parsons. A short time later, George Taylor called back and stated that as far as he could determine, Mrs. Parsons had not been to the Sammis property that day.

William decided it was time to call the police. His first call was to the state police substation in Port Jefferson. When no one picked up the phone, he hung up and dialed the number for the Brookhaven Town Police. Lieutenant Stacey Wilson answered the telephone. William simply said, "Stacey, can I see you?"

2
ALICE MCDONELL PARSONS

Alice W. McDonell, like most people, had both good and bad things happen throughout her short life. However, regardless of what was put before her, she always managed to maintain a bright disposition. She was considered by many of her schoolmates, friends and family to be a sweet, if somewhat gullible, soul.

Her life began on May 3, 1898, in Bay City, Michigan. Her mother, Alice Williams McDonell, and her father, Frank McDonell, originally hailed from Rye, New York. Her father appeared to move quite often and held addresses on Wapponoca Avenue in Rye and on East 26th Street and East 95th Street in New York City. There are records indicating that he spent some time in Canada. Alice had two brothers of whom she was very fond, Frank Jr. and Howard McDonell. The first tragedy in Alice's life occurred at the tender age of six years, when her mother died of peritonitis following a miscarriage. Alice's father determined early on that he was ill-equipped to raise a daughter and turned to his deceased wife's brother for help. That man was Colonel Timothy S. Williams. The loving and generous Uncle Timothy became one of the most important people in Alice's life and, perhaps tangentially, a contributing factor in her early and tragic death.

Colonel Timothy S. Williams began his career as a newspaper reporter in Washington, D.C. He was a graduate of Cornell University, and while covering stories in Washington, he became a favorite at President Cleveland's White House. His dealings with politicians eventually led to his obtaining a position in New York's governing circles, where he became the private

Left: Alice Williams McDonell, mother of Alice McDonell Parsons. She died from peritonitis in 1904 following a miscarriage. *Author's collection.*

Right: Frank McDonell, father of Alice McDonell Parsons. *Author's collection.*

secretary to Governor David B. Hill. He was such a pronounced success in the position that when Roswell P. Flower succeeded Hill as governor, Flower kept Colonel Williams in his position. Governor Flower liked Colonel Williams so much that he eventually gave him a position within Flower's Brooklyn Rapid Transit Company. Later in life, Colonel Williams would become the president of that company.

As a successful railroad man in the early part of the twentieth century, Colonel Williams was considered to be both wealthy and powerful. However, throughout his life, the thing that appeared to be the dearest to Colonel Williams was his family. Colonel Williams married Alice Kelley in 1895. She brought a child named Edna with her to the marriage; however, Colonel Williams and Alice Kelley never had a child together. It was clear by his actions over the years that he truly adored his wife and his sisters Alice and Bess. When his sister Alice died, he agreed to assume the guardianship of his niece, Alice McDonell.

Although Alice's brothers, Frank Jr. and Howard, were technically under the care of their father, Uncle Timothy kept a close watch on them as

Left: Colonel Timothy Williams was uncle, benefactor and legal guardian to Alice McDonell Parsons. *Author's collection.*

Right: Alice's aunt Bessie Williams took over the role of Alice's mother and helped raise Alice at Colonel Williams's Shoreland estate. *Author's collection.*

well. There were many letters and notes exchanged over the years between Colonel Williams and the male members of the McDonell family. One of the most telling letters was one sent by Colonel Williams to Alice's father on May 20, 1911. It read:

> *Mr. Frank D. McDonell*
> *High River, Alberta,*
> *Canada*
>
> *My Dear Frank,*
>
> *I received your telegram of the 16th instant and also your previous letter dated Bay City, but delayed in transmission.*
> *I confess I do not know what has gotten into your head.*
> *In the first place I have no property of the boys in my possession. If you are under the impression that they are beneficiaries under my Aunt Harriet's Will you are entirely mistaken. They were cited for the probate of the Will*

as required by the law because they were among the next of kin, but they are not participants under the Will directly or indirectly. If you refer to the fund which I have set aside from my own possessions for the ultimate benefit of the boys and their sister, I say frankly that I have not the least intention of turning that fund over to you or to anybody else for investment. It does not become their property until I choose to make it so, and until that time I propose to handle it myself.

Very truly yours,
Timothy S. Williams

Other letters, notes and telegrams sent over the years between Uncle Timothy and Alice's brothers made it clear that he was sending the brothers allowances, paying for their educations and helping them with their eventual careers. Alice was certainly not forgotten. She was sent to the best schools, which included Miss Porter's School in Farmington, Connecticut. Miss Porter's School was considered one of the most elite schools for young ladies at that time. It was established in 1843 by education reformer Sarah Porter, who recognized the importance of women's education. Alice's curriculum included chemistry, physiology, botany, geology and astronomy in addition to the more traditional Latin, French, German, spelling, reading, arithmetic,

Howard, Alice and Frank Jr. McDonell in an early childhood photo. All three siblings remained close through the years. *Author's collection.*

Shoreland was built by Colonel Timothy Williams in 1905 and became Alice's home after her mother's death in 1904. Alice and William were married in this home. *From the Col. Timothy Williams Letters Collection, New York City Library.*

trigonometry, history and geography. Once Alice's formal schooling was complete, Uncle Timothy rounded out her education by sending her on an extended trip through Europe.

Although Alice did not appear to have a close relationship with her father, they remained in contact and visited each other on occasion over the years. This included a trip by Alice to Alberta, Canada, to visit her father and later a visit to Long Meadow Farm by her father and his second wife, Grace.

In 1902, Colonel Williams purchased one hundred acres of land at West Neck Avenue in Huntington from Warren B. Sammis, with the intention of building a large estate. The land had a breathtaking view of both Cold Spring Harbor and Long Island Sound. Three years later, Williams's construction on the property was complete, and the Shoreland Estate was born. The newly constructed main residence included a bowling alley, a twenty-four-by-seventy-six-foot billiard room, a wine closet and an electric passenger elevator. There were verandas surrounding the house, leaded glass windows and a stable to accommodate ten horses, as well as coachman's and gardener's quarters.

Colonel Williams and his wife became active participants in community affairs, which included his serving as a director of the Huntington Hospital

Alice Parsons in her younger years. *Author's collection.*

Association and chairman of the board of the Long Island Biological Association, which later became part of the Cold Spring Harbor Laboratory. In his later years, Colonel Williams spent much of his time at his Shoreland estate.

This magnificent location was chosen as the venue for Alice's wedding. On November 1, 1925, after an engagement of just a few months, Alice McDonell married William H. Parsons Jr. She was twenty-eight years old. They honeymooned in Rio de Janeiro and Cuba.

Upon returning from their honeymoon, William and Alice moved into a single room above the garage at William's father's Glen Cove country estate. Three years later, on April 30, 1928, William and Alice purchased the twenty-two-acre Long Meadow Farm in Stony Brook from John Lewis Childs for $12,000. Present during the negotiations was Uncle Timothy, who would hold a mortgage of $10,500.

Just nine months after Alice's Shoreland Estate wedding, Uncle Timothy was stricken with a cerebral hemorrhage. He survived that ordeal only to succumb to a heart attack four years later in the apartment of a Mrs. Maude Lawrence of 220 West 107th Street in Manhattan. Although never substantiated, several family members believed that this address maintained a house of ill repute.

The provisions of Colonel Timothy S. Williams's will would eventually make Alice Parsons a rich woman. The first phase of the will established an immediate trust of $30,000 for Alice, the principal and interest of which became available to her on her thirty-fifth birthday. The death of Alice W. Williams, Colonel Williams's wife, due to pneumonia in 1936 and the subsequent sale of portions of the Shoreland estate resulted in an additional inheritance for Alice and the promise of future funds.

However, a dark cloud hung over both Colonel Williams's and his wife's wills: Edna Kelley, who was Mrs. Williams's daughter from a previous marriage. Edna Kelley had been completely left out of any interest in the Shoreland estate, where she had lived most of her life. In the end, the bulk of the Shoreland estate would go to Colonel Williams's sister Bess Williams and his niece Alice Parsons. It was reported at the time that Edna Kelley and Bess Williams were bitter enemies, while Bess Williams and Alice Parsons were the best of friends. Part of the issue regarding Edna Kelley and the family had to do with her being committed to mental institutions on several occasions due to a recurring mental ailment. This included several stays at the Interlines Sanitarium in Goshen, New York, when she was twenty years of age.

Once Mrs. Williams died, both Edna Kelley and Bess Williams gave up the residence at Shoreland. It was reported that Kelley had intended to move into the Sammis place, but this move had been vetoed by both Bess Williams and Alice Parsons. Kelley eventually moved into a somewhat shabby residence in Huntington and was considered to be in a very difficult financial situation at the time of Alice's disappearance.

The exact amount of Alice Parsons's expected inheritance became an obsession with the press after her disappearance. A great many stories were printed, and each contained a varying dollar amount. However, it was officially determined at the time that on April 27, 1937, a small parcel sale of the estate netted Alice a total of $7,000, which she promptly added to her $30,000 trust. The remaining Shoreland estate was valued at $275,000, of which by the terms of her uncle's will Alice was entitled to 30 percent, or $82,500 ($1,480,000 in 2019 dollars). Alice also held a 30 percent share in the Sammis property in Huntington, which would eventually entitle her to an additional $8,000 when the property was sold.

On May 18, 1937, just twenty-two days before Alice's disappearance, an odd thing occurred. William and Alice visited the office of W.K. Allison of the law firm Cullen & Dyckman on Montague Street in Brooklyn, New York, and executed new wills. Alice's new will called for a direct bequest of $35,000 to be made to her husband, William H. Parsons Jr., upon her death and an outright gift of $10,000 to their housekeeper, Anna Kupryanova. The remainder of her property would be held in trust by the Brooklyn Trust Company, and the income generated from that property would go to her husband for the remainder of his life. After the death of her husband, two-thirds of the property in trust would go to Anna Kupryanova's son, Roy. The remaining third would go to the children of Alice's brother Frank Jr. and the soon-to-be-born child of her brother Howard McDonell.

Alice Parsons maintained relatively good health throughout her life. Newspaper reports at the time of her disappearance alluded to a serious childhood injury that resulted in her inability to have children. This, as with many of the things stated in the press at the time, was completely false.

There was no childhood injury or serious illness. However, Alice did appear to have a difficult time in becoming pregnant. When Alice and William first purchased the farm, Alice did all of the housework and cooking. She also helped William considerably in clearing the land and establishing the poultry livestock. Shortly after moving into Long Meadow Farm, Alice became increasingly concerned about her inability to become pregnant. She had been seeking treatment from doctors for this condition for four years. One of the doctors suggested that she may have been overstressing her body with physical work on the farm.

She and William then decided to hire a housekeeper. Several local women were tried, but for various reasons, they did not stay employed by the Parsonses for any length of time. This was the reason for employing Anna Kupryanova in March 1931.

Alice's inability to become pregnant and stay pregnant was a major issue in her and William's lives. On September 25, 1932, Alice met with Dr. Virgil Green Damon at his Park Avenue, New York City office. Dr. Damon had been recommended to Alice by her personal physician Dr. Frank Childs of Port Jefferson, New York. The letter of introduction sent by Alice's personal physician indicated that Alice was being sent to Dr. Damon because of sterility; it indicated that she had been married for seven years, without bearing any children, and that on December 21, 1930, Alice had suffered a miscarriage early in a pregnancy.

Dr. Damon found Alice to be of the quiet, phlegmatic type and not subject to nervousness or fits of depression. He noted that she exhibited a strong desire to have a child of her own and agreed to undergo a series of treatments. Dr. Damon noted in his file that his physical examination of Alice revealed a tipped uterus. Alice received at least six treatments from Dr. Damon, the last being in March 1933. Dr. Damon had also noted in his files that an examination of Alice's husband, William, showed no medical condition that would prevent him from impregnating his wife.

Alice eventually became discouraged with the lack of success, and in a September 1933 letter to Dr. Damon, she wrote:

> *Some time has elapsed since my last visit to your office and I want to apologize for having so abruptly stopped coming after your interest and care in my behalf. Perhaps I should explain that I have become too discouraged to keep on as I did not feel I ought to from the financial side as well.*
>
> *I want to thank you for your interest but I truly do not feel that there is much use in my entailing the expense. At any rate, in present times.*

Alice's love for children was quite evident to those around her. When their new housekeeper and her son, Roy, arrived at the Parsons farm in March 1931, Alice immediately began treating the then six-year-old boy as her own. She also frequently invited her nieces Alice and Florence to visit the farm during their summer recess.

The only instance when William and Alice were separated for any length of time was in the fall of 1936, when Alice traveled alone to California for her brother Howard's wedding to Jeane Marie Weber. Howard was a Columbia Studio executive at the time. Alice had looked forward to attending the wedding with her aunt Bessie. When an illness prevented her aunt from attending, Alice decided to go alone, although her aunt still paid for Alice's travel expenses for the cross-country train trip. When Alice arrived in Los Angeles, she stayed in the home of Mrs. Weber, her brother's soon-to-be mother-in-law. While in California, Alice also visited her father and stepmother. She even attended a social affair at the home of a distant cousin by the name of Mrs. Sinclair Gluck. Mrs. Gluck found Alice to be a quiet, "mouse-like" woman who was rather timid and could easily be persuaded by others. She also noted that Alice appeared to be happy and in high spirits. Alice's visit to California lasted two weeks. She then traveled by train to San Francisco with an acquaintance of hers by the name of Betsy Arnold. Once in San Francisco, Alice switched trains and began her long journey back to Long Island.

The day before Alice Parsons disappeared was a busy one for her. It started with her, William, Anna and Roy all having their usual breakfast together. Later in the morning, Arnold Cox made a delivery to the farm. Cox owned the business that collected the Parsonses' trash on Mondays, Wednesdays and Fridays. However, that day he was making a delivery of four bags of pigeon feed that William had ordered. Alice spoke with Cox for a short while as William prepared a check.

A short time later, Alice left the farm, drove to the Sinclair gas station in Stony Brook and purchased eight gallons of gasoline for her Dodge. She then stopped at the Three Village Tea House in Stony Brook. One of Alice's small income-generating projects was to grow plants and flowers and display them for sale at the Tea House. On occasion, she would also leave eggs, cakes, squab paste, kipper paste, French onion soup and mushroom soup for sale. In fact, Alice was the chairman of the Three Village Garden Club pantry committee, which placed food, plants and floral items for sale at the Tea Room. According to Alice's friend Mrs. Gowdey, Alice was in the habit of coming to the Three Village Tea House practically every day.

On this day, Alice had brought with her a large bouquet of yellow roses. When she greeted Mrs. Gowdey, she appeared to be in a jovial spirit and remarked jokingly that the roses were very beautiful and that she had never seen their equal. She remarked that the roses were the result of her efforts to develop an attractive garden. She then put the roses in a vase and left them in the Tea Room.

Mrs. Gowdey was the head of the Three Village Garden Club, one of the few community organizations that Alice actively participated in. The Garden Club was scheduled to meet the next day at the home of the influential and wealthy Mrs. Frank Melville. Alice had let it be known that she was anxious to attend. She had personally arranged for a special guest speaker from the New York Times Garden Section to address the club.

Mrs. Melville's home was a palatial estate in an area known as Old Field village. She had organized the Three Village Garden Club as a charitable organization five years prior, and it maintained over three hundred members. Mrs. Melville was acquainted with Alice and had held strong opinions on Alice's domestic situation, which included the presence of Anna Kupryanova in the Parsons home. Mrs. Melville went so far as to state that it was her belief that William Parsons was the father of the boy, Roy, brought to this country by their Russian housekeeper. It was an opinion held by many at the time.

While at the Tea House, Alice placed some plants for sale on the porch and spoke with Mrs. Walter Nevins. Mrs. Nevins described Alice as being "a snappy little thing—her eyes would snap and would fight for anything that belonged to her. She was a bubbly little woman, not in the least nervous about anything."

A short conversation ensued, and Mrs. Nevins told Alice that she was interested in purchasing a plant from her known as the "Hardy Veronica." Anna told her she would bring the plant to Mrs. Nevins's home the very next day—Wednesday, June 9, 1937, the day of Alice's disappearance.

Sometime after visiting the Tea Room for lunch that afternoon, Alice visited the Emma S. Clark Memorial Library in Setauket. According to the librarian, Martha Basten, Alice was in the library for approximately twenty minutes. Alice had requested two books: *They Walk in the City* by J.B. Priestley and *Beyond Sing the Woods* by Trygve Gulbranssen. Both of these books were out, so Alice asked Mrs. Basten to reserve them for her when they returned. Alice then took out *Heritage* by George F. Hummel and *My Ten Years in a Quandary* by Robert Benchley. Alice also took out several books for Roy, whom she often referred to as her adopted son. Alice also mentioned to Mrs.

Basten that she and her husband intended to send Roy to the Stony Brook School for Boys in the fall.

Later that afternoon, William and Alice drove together to Huntington to meet with Frederick Hubbs about painting several rooms at the newly rented Sammis place. Hubbs had done the original paint job on the Sammis estate about twenty-five years ago. Alice informed him of the work she needed done and requested an estimate. The three of them then proceeded to the Sammis place to view the rooms that needed painting. Hubbs indicated that Alice was in a very good mood that day. Once Hubbs looked over the rooms, he quoted Alice a price of twenty-five dollars. Alice told him she would send him a note telling him if his price was acceptable and when he could begin the work.

After visiting the Sammis place with Hubbs, William and Alice returned to their farm late in the afternoon. It was then that they discussed further the meeting that Anna Kupryanova had arranged for William in New York City for the very next day.

3
WILLIAM H. PARSONS JR.

William H. Parsons Jr. was forty-nine years old in 1937. He was the son of W.H. Parsons, a wealthy industrialist who had done business around the world and was president of W.H. Parsons & Company, a New York City–based paper manufacturing business. The senior Parsons was also well known as a militant crusader against obscenity and vice in New York City. For twenty-three years, he served as an officer and eventually as president of the New York Society for the Suppression of Vice, helping to build the organization into an auxiliary arm of the New York Police Department, joining its war on lewdness and immorality.

William was the oldest of five. His brothers were John Palmer Parsons of Bayside, New York, and Oliver Walcott Parsons of Carpinteria, California. His sisters were Laura W. Pratt of Glen Cove, New York, and Mary Marselis Parsons, who resided with her father at 129 East 69th Street in New York City until his death in 1935. Mary was affectionately known to her siblings as Molly.

William attended the Hill School in Pottstown, Pennsylvania, and later Yale University. While at Yale, he was a member of the Psi Upsilon fraternity and graduated from the university in 1910. He later joined the U.S. Navy and served from April 1917 to December 1918. At the time of his discharge he was a lieutenant, junior grade. Upon his honorable discharge, he joined his father's paper manufacturing company.

William acted as the company's representative in London from mid-1923 to January 1925. According to Emily McDonell, the wife of Alice's

William H. Parsons Jr. addressing reporters outside of his farmhouse shortly after Alice's kidnapping. *Author's collection.*

brother Frank Jr., she (Emily) met William when he was working for his father's company in England. According to Emily, William had been asked by his landlords to move—on several occasions—due to his escapades with women. These escapades included a love affair with a young woman by the name of Mary Thomas, who, it was reported, later married an Englishman sometime after William returned to the United States.

There had been a great deal of speculation in both the community and the press, both before and after the disappearance of Alice Parsons, as to the possibility of William Parsons being the natural father of Anna Kupryanova's son, Roy. One newspaper falsely reported that the police had determined that William Parsons and Anna Kupryanova knew each other in England, when, in fact, there was no evidence that they had ever met while he was in England. According to available records, William Parsons left England in January 1925, and Roy was not even conceived until the following October, with a recorded birth in June 1926.

Upon returning to New York, William was introduced to Alice McDonell. Both of their families had lived in Rye, New York, and it was inevitable that the two should meet someday.

After William and Alice married, they lived together at his father's country estate for several years. William continued to work for his father's company. However, after a period of time, he began to have difficulty getting along with one of the younger members of the company and decided to leave the company in the spring of 1927. He had decided over the course of

Long Meadow farmhouse photo taken shortly after the kidnapping. Three Brookhaven Town policemen can be seen standing on the property. *Courtesy of Three Village Historical Society.*

the summer of that year that it would be best if he returned to work at his father's paper company in the fall. However, he had recently become interested in poultry and agriculture due to his activity in helping around his father's estate. He then took an agriculture course during the following winter and decided on a career in farming.

On April 20, 1928, real estate broker Charles E. Powel of Stony Brook, Long Island, sold a home and twenty-two acres of land belonging to John Lewis Childs to William H. Parsons Jr. for $12,000. The property stood on Gould Road in Stony Brook and was known as Long Meadow Farm.

The day before Alice Parsons disappeared, her husband, William, busied himself with various chores and errands. One of his first morning tasks was to pay Arnold Cox for delivering four bags of grit he had ordered. He later visited W.B. Ketchum at the Stony Brook railway station. Ketchum was the shipping agent for Railway Express, the Long Island Rail Road and Western Union. William had brought with him a tub of dressed squabs to be delivered to an address on 14th Street in New York City. William also mentioned that he was expecting a large package containing a broken farm wagon, and he requested that Ketchum hold the item at the station and not deliver it to the farm. William stated that he wanted to take the wagon directly to a local shop for repairs before bringing it home.

Later that afternoon, William drove Alice to Huntington for her meeting with Frederick Hubbs. For the last several months, all issues regarding the Shoreland Estate and the Sammis place had been handled strictly by Alice. Although William had heard of Hubbs, they had never met. After Hubbs and William inspected the rooms at the Sammis place that were to be painted, William and Alice returned to their farm in Stony Brook. There William, Alice, Anna and Roy had their final dinner together.

4
ANNA KUPRYANOVA

Anna Kupryanova was William and Alice Parsons's housekeeper. Anna's maiden name was Shishoff, and she was born in Yalta, Crimea, Russia, on February 4, 1901. Her mother was Emily Wolff Shishoff, and her father was Stanislaw Shishoff. Anna also had a brother who was the director of an agricultural school in Cherson. He was reportedly killed by the Bolsheviks in 1918. Her mother and married sister continued to live in an area known as Simferopol, Crimea. Unfortunately, due to the location and the period, there are few records that document the early years of Anna's life. There is some indication that she may have been married at the age of seventeen to a man named Potocky. The marriage lasted only a few months due to an accident in which Potocky was killed. This incident reportedly took place in Tiflis, Caucasia, Russia.

When Anna was nineteen years old and studying biology at the local university, she met Alexander Kupryanova. They were introduced through her sister-in-law. Alexander was attached to the Russian army at the time, and after a courtship of just a few months, they married. The wedding took place in Novorossiysk on the coast of the Black Sea. For an unknown reason, Anna quit the university shortly after her marriage to Alexander. Russia was a turbulent place at the time, and Anna and her husband decided to leave the country and flee to Constantinople, Turkey, as refugees. From Turkey, they moved to Yugoslavia and remained there for two years. It was reported that in 1923, during their time together in Yugoslavia, Anna gave birth to a daughter she named Melochka, but the child died within a year. In May of that same year, Alexander Kupryanova left Yugoslavia for America, and Anna remained behind.

The following February, Anna obtained a passport in Zagreb, Croatia, with the intent of permanently rejoining her husband in America. Alexander had sent her a one-way steamship ticket to New York, and on March 12, 1924, Anna arrived in the Port of New York aboard the SS *Aquitania*. She was reportedly visited by her husband while she was waiting for her immigration clearance. Unfortunately, her stay in America was a short one. When questioned at Ellis Island by the Board of Special Inquiry, Anna insisted that her teaching skills, although limited, exempted her from the current Russian immigration quota. Members of the board did not agree with her; on March 24, 1924, they issued their final ruling and Anna Kupryanova

Anna Kupryanova had this professional photograph taken and distributed to the press after she became a suspect in Alice's disappearance. *Courtesy of Three Village Historical Society.*

was deported. On March 29, 1924, Anna boarded the SS *Franconia* of the Cunard Line, which was destined for Southampton, England. Upon arrival in England, Anna was placed in a camp in Atlantic Park, at Eastley, at the expense of the Cunard Line.

Anna was unhappy with both the people and the surroundings at the Atlantic Park camp, and after one year, she left for West Kensington. After leaving the camp, Anna moved to several different residences during the period between 1925 and 1926. These included 11 Gunterson Road, West Kensington; 46 Charleville Road, West Kensington; 6 Wavedon Road, Kew Gardens; and 3 Defoe Avenue, Kew Gardens.

In early 1926, Anna met an Indian man named Hans Soni in London. Soni had come to England in 1918 to further his education in economics. He graduated with a master's degree from Edinburgh University in 1923 and had been conducting research on different aspects of economics at the London School of Economics and Political Science. Soni returned home to Punjab, India, after he received his degree and remained there for approximately two years. He again traveled to London in early 1926 and secured a position as a clerk in the Office of the Trade Commissioner for India in Chiswick, London, where he met Anna Kupryanova. Within a very short period, they moved into a residence together in West Kensington.

A short time after Anna and Soni met, Anna wrote to her husband, Alexander, in an act of contrition as well as desperation. Her letter, originally written in Russian, was translated into English and made part of Alexander Kupryanova's divorce petition. The letter reads as follows:

Dear Shura [short for Alexander]

I wanted to write to you about this two months ago but it was so hard that I couldn't possible do it. Now, however, I feel that I have no right to deceive you and I must tell you about it all frankly. I know it will be very hard for you, insulting and disgraceful but you must remember that I have always been a good wife, and shared your trouble as well as your joy. I have sinned but who does not sin? I want to talk this over with you as with a friend and not as an insulted husband. Do this last thing for me.

I have been faithless to you and now this is my second month of pregnancy: I feel bad, I am ill, and beg of you only one thing; to help me in the name of our past and in the name of Melochka. Think of the life we have spent; of the trouble we have had at that time when she was to have been born; and all this I have to go through now by myself knowing that my coming child will be illegal. If you ever did love me you will help me now. I know I have brought you much pain, but Shura, you are young, it will all be forgotten; you will find your happiness. It is true it will be hard at the beginning and it probably will seem impossible, but what wound does not heal? Nobody will ever know that we have ever suffered so much. It will be better for you to remember that your wife has been an honest woman; that she told you frankly of her being faithless. You know yourself that it is hard when once you have slipped from the straight way, but I have slipped and I feel it now; it is immaterial, and it seems so hard to me. Do not scold me, do not taunt me, it would not help any more. Just look at it logically: one has sinned and it cannot be helped. They will probably not let me enter into the United States and I myself do not want to go there. I do not want to disgrace you in the eyes of your friends. They will never know anything about it. You just tell them that your wife has been ill and later died: all will be forgotten. I will never trod on our path any longer. I ask of you only one thing: help me to go to my mother. You see the Cunard Company will keep me here and you would probably have to support me here and then also my child and all the expenses to be paid. You see you cannot leave me on the English territory. I will ask you just to this thing for me and make an end of it. Go to the Court and tell them that your wife has deceived you;

that she was faithless to you. If you want I may write you an official letter about it; and that therefore you want to divorce her. They will undoubtedly give you a divorce. You may send me a copy of same. I will get my passport on my maiden name and go to my mother. I have written to her to get for me a passport there. She has promised to do so but I have to go there on my maiden name, otherwise they would want to know where you are and where you live so there would probably be a lot of unpleasantness for you and also for your father on account of it. You understand that under the laws of the Soviet Government I could get a divorce in twenty-four hours, but I do want to part from you as friends. You understand of course, that in the future I will live for my child only, as I have nothing else in life to look forward to. Think about it all. Do not be angry but try to understand that a person is not always liable for his acts, that sometimes fate plays with him. I will beg you once again do all I ask you to do and don't tell anybody about it and no one will know. I will leave as soon as I get my passport on my maiden name and play our part to the end. You will send me money for my way back. You know that I haven't a cent. In the name of our past you will do this for me and do it as soon as you can. It is very hard for me, Shura, I know that I have caused you great pain, that you are an ideal husband, but I have been bad. I will wish you the best of happiness; I know you deserve it and not matter how hard it will be it will all be forgotten.

There is one more thing I will ask you for. Do not think of my [sic] *badly. I suffered a great deal physically and mentally. I realize now how bad I have been but cannot help it. We will have to end it all. I will ask you once again not to be angry and not to scold me. Try to understand what happened. Consider me unfortunate and help me in the name of our past and in the name of our Melochka.*

Anya

Very shortly after Anna and Hans Soni met, he became aware that she was expecting a child. In May 1926, two significant events occurred in Anna's life. First, Alexander's petition for divorce was granted by the Court of Common Pleas, Cuyahoga County, Cleveland, Ohio. Second, Anna and Hans moved into their Defoe Avenue home in Kew Gardens. Two weeks later, Anna gave birth to a son. Although Hans Soni accepted the male child, he refused to accept the fact that he was the father. The fact that the child had to have been conceived the previous fall, several months before they had met each other, convinced him that he was not the boy's father. He went so

Certified copy of Roy's birth certificate from the General Registry Office, Somerset House, London, England. *From the National Archives.*

far as to state at a later date that he had no idea who the father of the child was and that she was a Russian refugee and had been in "liaison" with a number of men.

Hans Soni's denial of paternity did not stop Anna from claiming so on the birth records of her new son. The birth registration in Richmond, in the County of Surrey in July 1926, indicated that Roy Chandra was born on June 12, 1926. The registration indicates that the birth took place at the residence located at 3 Defoe Avenue. The name of the father was listed as Hans Roy Soni, student of economics. The mother's name was listed as Ina Soni, formerly Kuprianov.

Approximately two years later, in 1928, Hans Soni left Anna and her son and returned to India. He joined the territorial staff of Hindu College at Delhi. It was not long before he stopped sending money to Anna. Anna was facing difficult times with few friends and virtually no resources. She was forced to sell her few possessions, and in the fall of 1928, she moved into the home of a sympathetic couple by the name of Haydn and Marie Houlgate. Mr. Houlgate was an employee of the U.S. State Department. Anna, Roy and the Houlgates shared the residence for four months until Anna was able to secure a position as housekeeper with Mrs. Amy Shakespeare at 61 Philbeach Gardens, London. Hans Soni had his last contact with Anna in 1930, when she reached out and begged him for money so that she could travel to the United States.

Anna procured all of the necessary visa applications from the U.S. Consul in London. When she completed the application, she was issued visa number 2219. Her application stated that she was married to Alexander

Kupryanova of Bridgeport, Connecticut, and that Alexander was the father of Roy Chandra Kupryanova.

On June 5, 1930, Anna Kupryanova and her son, Roy, stepped off the Cunard Line's SS *Mauretania* at the Port of New York. She was met at the ship by her former husband, Alexander. Alexander brought Anna and Roy to his small furnished apartment in Bridgeport, Connecticut, where Alexander was working for the Sikorsky Corporation. Two months after Anna's arrival, she opened a small rooming house with money furnished by Alexander. The venture failed quickly, and Anna decided to try her luck in New York City.

On September 2, 1930, Anna arrived in New York City and went directly to the International Institute of the YWCA. There she met with a social worker by the name of Kyra Malkovsky. Malkovsky arranged housing for Anna and Roy, and they moved into a home on 205th Street in Bayside, Queens. Anna's first job in New York City was as a housekeeper for Mrs. Bryan Eagles. The position did not allow Anna to bring young Roy to work with her. This was of deep concern to Anna, and she began looking for a different position almost immediately. Coincidentally, Kyra Malkovsky and Laura Pratt, the sister of William Parsons, were friends. Anna Kupryanova's situation was discussed, and Laura Pratt suggested that her brother might be looking for a housekeeper at his farm on Long Island. On March 23, 1931, Anna Kupryanova and Roy moved to Long Meadow Farm.

Anna Kupryanova began calling herself Anna Cooper sometime after she moved into the Parsons residence. She felt at the time that many people were having difficulty pronouncing her last name and that the name *Cooper* was close enough to satisfy everyone. In June 1932, Anna filed her Declaration of Intention to become a citizen in the U.S. District Court in Brooklyn. The two witnesses on her application were the social worker Kyra Malkovsky and a bookkeeper by the name of Matislav Golovan of Bayside, New York. In this application, Anna requested that her name be changed from Anna Kupryanova to Anna Cooper. A similar request had been made to the local school authorities in Stony Brook, and young Roy would henceforth be known as Roy Cooper.

Anna became a U.S. citizen on July 7, 1936. This was just eleven months before the disappearance of Alice Parsons. To the shock and surprise of both William's and Alice's families, Anna was granted permission by the Parsonses to amend her citizen application and change her last name from the requested Cooper to Parsons. Young Roy's records were also changed, and both he and Anna became new members of the Parsons family.

Anna Kupryanova's son, Roy, bringing milk into the farmhouse. Roy was moved to William's sister Laura Pratt's home in Glen Cove, Long Island, shortly after Alice's kidnapping. *Courtesy of Three Village Historical Society.*

Two weeks before Alice's disappearance, Anna wrote to her friend Kyra Malkovsky in New York City, asking Kyra to arrange a meeting with Baron George Touve of the Russian caviar distribution company Macoroff, in order to obtain advice that would assist the Parsonses in the marketing and distribution of their squab paste. Anna had suggested a proposed meeting date in the letter. Although she did not hear back from Kyra, Anna went into New York City on that date. She was driven to the train station by William, and she left on the 7:46 a.m. train. Unfortunately, Anna missed a letter delivered to the farm that very day indicating that Kyra would be out of town. When Anna arrived at Kyra Malkovsky's YWCA office in Manhattan, she was informed that Malkovsky was out of town. Anna then met with her friend Mrs. Golovan. They had lunch together and attended a picture show. A few days later, Kyra returned to the city and communicated to Anna that she would arrange a meeting with Touve.

On June 8, 1937, the day before Alice Parsons's disappearance, Anna received a telephone call from Kyra Malkovsky telling her that the meeting she had requested with Touve had been arranged for 11:30 a.m. the very next day. The meeting was to take place at the Grand Central Palace in New York City. When told of the arranged meeting, William Parsons decided that he would handle this meeting alone.

5

THE INVESTIGATION BEGINS

In the early evening of June 9, 1937, Brookhaven Township Police lieutenant Stacey Wilson answered his office telephone and heard William Parsons say, "Stacey, can I see you?"

He immediately asked William Parsons what this was about. William simply answered that he could not talk about it over the telephone but that it was in reference to Mrs. Parsons.

Lieutenant Wilson and Officer Fitzpatrick arrived at Long Meadow Farm at approximately 7:45 p.m. They were met by William Parsons, who told them that his wife had been supposed to meet him at the Huntington train station that evening and that she had not shown up. William said that he had called his home and spoken to Anna and she had informed him that Mrs. Parsons had gone to Huntington. William said that after talking with Anna, he took the next train home. When he arrived home, Anna had advised him that Mrs. Parsons had gone to the Sammis place in Huntington earlier in the day. He told Lieutenant Wilson that the Sammis place was soon to be rented to a Mrs. Burdin and that Alice may have gone there to show the property to someone. When Lieutenant Wilson inquired as to the necessity of showing the property if it had already been rented, Anna interrupted and said Mrs. Burdin wanted an oil burner and Mrs. Parsons thought she might be able to lease the property without installing one.

At that point, Lieutenant Wilson asked who Anna was.

William Parsons said, "Wilson, this is my sister. You can call her Miss Parsons." It was the very first lie in a long list of lies that would be spoken that evening.

Lieutenant Wilson questioned Anna about what she saw, heard and did that day. He then asked her to reenact the events that led to Mrs. Parsons's absence from the farm. Anna explained that she and Alice were in the kitchen fixing a gosling's injured leg when a shiny black car that looked like a Buick drove up to the house. Mrs. Parsons walked out to the car to greet the visitors, and Anna followed her out the door and went to the pigeon house. Anna estimated the time to be about 10:45 a.m. As Anna was heading to the pigeon house, she saw Mrs. Parsons leaning on the car; a man was seated behind the steering wheel, and a woman was sitting beside him.

Anna remembered that Alice was wearing an apron, brown shoes and stockings. Anna then stated that about fifteen minutes later, Mrs. Parsons entered the pigeon house and was all dressed up. She was now wearing a blue dress with red buttons. The top of the dress had blue polka dots. She was also wearing a soft blue felt hat and carried a beaded pocketbook. Anna was not certain about the type of shoes Alice was wearing. Alice had said that the people in the automobile were going to take her over to the Sammis place in order that she might show that place to an elderly lady who was there. Anna said that Alice had told her that she would be home for lunch. Anna then told Lieutenant Wilson that the visitors' car was parked immediately adjacent to the Parsons' Dodge and that the Dodge was in the same place next to the house where Alice had parked it when she had returned from taking William to the train station that morning. In one of the more inexplicable and conflicting statements that Anna made, she stated to Lieutenant Wilson that she was unable to give any description of the people in the car because she had not paid them any attention.

Anna stated that she left the pigeon house shortly after Alice did and had seen the visitors' car as it left the driveway. She stated that the man was driving and Alice and the woman were sitting in the back seat. Once the car left the driveway, it turned left and headed in a southerly direction on the main road.

Lieutenant Wilson's questioning of William and Anna took approximately fifteen minutes. He then suggested to William Parsons that he contact relatives to see if Alice had visited them. He asked Anna to show him the gosling she had been tending when the visitors arrived approximately nine hours earlier. Anna pulled up a cover on the kitchen table to reveal a basket containing a dead gosling. Anna seemed quite surprised that the gosling was dead. Lieutenant Wilson noted that there was a half-filled two-ounce bottle of liquid sitting next to the basket. He noted the label on the bottle, which said, "Kane's Drug Store; Port Jefferson; Chloroform."

Officer Fitzpatrick began to ask Anna some follow-up questions. Lieutenant Wilson took that opportunity to slip up the stairs and conduct a short interview with young Roy Parsons, who was in his room. Roy told Lieutenant Wilson that the last time he had seen Mrs. Parsons was that morning at breakfast just before he had gone to school. He would later change his statement.

When Lieutenant Wilson finished speaking with Roy, he immediately returned downstairs to the kitchen. The first thing he noticed was that the bottle of chloroform was gone.

Lieutenant Wilson then called the Huntington Town Police and requested they check up on any reports of accidents possibly involving Mrs. Parsons. This was followed by a call to his chief of police. Investigator Bertram M. Walker of the Suffolk County District Attorney's Office was then called, and Lieutenant Wilson requested that he contact the Burdins to determine if Mrs. Parsons had gone to the Sammis place that day. As a result of this telephone call, numerous officers from various agencies began to appear at the farm. Among those were Brookhaven Police chief Edward Bridges, fingerprint expert John Harding and District Attorney's Office investigator Albert Kehlenbach.

During the course of his conversations with William and Anna, Lieutenant Wilson attempted to determine how much money William could afford to pay should this turn out to be a kidnapping case. It was at this point that Anna stated the police should go outside the house and look for a ransom note.

William, after a brief private conversation with Anna, asked Lieutenant Wilson to leave his house with his men and said that he was greatly concerned about getting bad publicity over this incident. He also stated that if this had been a kidnapping there must be a note.

Lieutenant Wilson, somewhat surprised at William's statement, asked him directly, "What makes you think this is a kidnapping? Your wife may be sick, or she may have fainted somewhere."

Parsons replied that his wife was never sick a day in her life.

Lieutenant Wilson informed William that his men were not leaving the house and asked him if it would be all right to call in a federal man. William stated he would rather he didn't because he did not want the publicity. A short time later, William told Wilson to use his own judgment regarding calling in the federal authorities.

John Harding of the Brookhaven Police Department was the second person to question William and Anna that evening. As was the case in the initial interview conducted by Lieutenant Wilson, William and Anna were questioned together. This initial interview took place in the dining room. Anna made several claims during this interview, including the fact that the Parsonses had adopted her son and that her husband was dead. After a short break, the interview was continued in William Parsons's office.

When Anna was asked what she thought had happened to Alice Parsons, she replied, "Well, she must be kidnapped." When questioned about why someone would want to kidnap Alice, she replied, "Well, for ransom, you know she is coming into a fortune."

William interrupted, "Fortune? Oh, it is not a fortune."

Anna replied, "Yes, Bill. It is a fortune."

When William was asked who knew that he was going into New York City that day, he replied, "Just Anna, my wife and I." He also stated that he had not made up his own mind to go until yesterday afternoon. When asked how often he traveled into New York City, he replied, "Three or four times a year, not more than that." When William was questioned about Anna's full name, he replied, "Well, she uses our name, Anna Parsons, Mrs. Parsons."

Harding asked, "Mrs. Parsons or Miss Parsons?"

William replied, "Mrs. Parsons."

Harding continued his questioning and asked William about Roy. When asked by Harding if he had adopted Anna's boy, William replied, "Yes." Harding then asked, "Legally?" and William again replied, "Yes."

William was then asked, "Have you ever done any cheating or stepping out or had any relations or correspondence with any other woman which your wife could possibly have learned about and cause her to leave you?"

William replied, "That's a very fair question. I see your point, but no, absolutely no. My wife and I lived perfectly. Nothing like that."

This question was followed by, "Are you sure that you and your wife have had no argument whatsoever that would possibly cause her to flare up and leave you?"

William answered, "I am sure. We never had an argument."

Investigator Kehlenbach was present during most of the questioning of William and Anna. In fact, he sat directly across from Anna at the kitchen table. He would later note that all during the questioning, Anna wore a smirk on her face and continually interrupted the questioning of William by stating that Alice must have been kidnapped.

During the course of the evening, Anna told Lieutenant Wilson numerous times that he should go outside and look for a note. She even made several suggestions as to where he should look. Wilson finally did go outside and checked various areas around the exterior of the house. At approximately 11:00 p.m., he checked the Parsonses' Dodge. Using a five-cell flashlight he checked the front and back seats and all of the floorboards.

His search did not produce a note.

Sometime before 11:30 p.m., Investigator Kehlenbach completed a search of the chicken coops and cistern. He then decided to search the Dodge. He was well aware that Lieutenant Wilson had already conducted a search of the vehicle. However, such repeated searches are not uncommon at crime scenes, and to this day, it is normally encouraged by fellow officers. Investigator Kehlenbach used his flashlight and examined the floor and seats of the front and back of the vehicle. There was no sign of any potential evidence.

At approximately 11:45 p.m., Investigator Bert Walker arrived at the Parsons home and advised Lieutenant Wilson that his investigation had failed to place Alice Parsons in or around the Sammis place that day. It was at about this time in the late evening that a Missing Persons Alarm was issued for Alice Parsons.

The alarm read as follows:

> *June 9th, 1937*
> *Alice Parsons, age 38—5'—135 lbs. Inlay work on teeth.*
> *Navy blue dress with red button on front—blue hat—grey eyes,*
> *Dark hair streaked with grey—ruddy complexion—round face, tan shoes*
> *and stockings—Left this a.m. in a large dark sedan possibly a Buick*
> *accompanied by a man and a woman and left in a southerly direction on*
> *Lake Grove Road towards Middle Country Road at Lake Grove*

It must be noted that at this point the criminal investigation into the disappearance of Alice Parsons was only four hours old and there had been nine major lies told to the police.

JUNE 10, 1937

Early Morning

Additional law enforcement personnel began arriving after midnight. These included Assistant District Attorney Brenner and Investigator Harvey Morris, as well as New York State Trooper Sullivan. Those already present were: Chief Bridges, Lieutenant Wilson, Fingerprint Specialist Harding, Investigator Walker and Investigator Kehlenbach. In the early hours of the morning, there were eight law enforcement officials, two adults and one sleeping child present at Long Meadow Farm. Those numbers would grow exponentially as dawn approached.

During the early hours of June 10, Chief Bridges began searching both the interior of the house and the surrounding grounds. During his search, he found two axes. One of the axes was in the chicken coop. It was approximately two feet in length and sported several dark clots that appeared to be blood. An examination of the blade indicated the presence of several short hairs. The second axe was found in the basement of the house. This axe was approximately three feet long and appeared to have dirt on the blade. Each of these items was placed uncovered on the floor of Chief Bridges's personal car. As was the case with each piece of potential evidence recovered at the Parsons farm that evening, no crime scene photographs were taken of these items before or after they were removed from their original locations.

At approximately 1:00 a.m., Anna was interviewed by Investigator Morris of the District Attorney's Office. In this interview, Anna claimed that her husband had been killed in an accident in Serbia in 1936 and that she had moved to England and married an Englishman. In one of her more telling statements, she said, "I am a woman of culture and nobility and believe that Mrs. Parsons was a woman of inferior complex, while I have a superiority complex." Speaking of Alice in the past tense, she said, "She just didn't seem to know how to run a home, so she was guided by my ideas at all times and so was Mr. Parsons."

Anna also stated that no one had come onto the premises, with the exception of her son, from the time Mrs. Parsons left with the two visitors until William Parsons returned home that evening. When Anna was asked if she had any concern at the time about Alice going away with two strangers, she replied, "She thought she was doing something smart, if she rented the house without telling me, and later should come home and brag about it."

Anna was then asked, "Have you ever cohabited with Mr. Parsons?"

Anna replied, "No."

Morris then asked, "Now, is that as true as everything else you have told me?"

Anna replied, "Yes."

Investigator Morris then interviewed William Parsons. During this interview, the first hint of domestic problems between William and Alice came to light. In contrast to the statement he had made to Brookhaven Police Department's John Harding just a few hours earlier, William revealed that during the previous six to eight weeks, his wife had not spoken to him sometimes for half a day at a time. This trouble, he asserted, arose over Anna—the other woman. He stated that he believed Anna was a brighter woman than his wife and had taken charge of the home and garden.

Morris then posed a critical question; he asked if Anna drove a car. William replied, "No, she was just beginning to learn."

During this interview, William Parsons claimed that Anna Kupryanova had been with the family for six or seven years and that he had personally gone into New York City and met Anna at the ocean liner. He claimed he had then brought her to the farm.

Then the subject of Alice's will was brought up. Investigator Morris asked William if he was aware of the contents of Alice's will. He said he was aware of the will's contents and that the will was only recently made. He explained that he was to receive the residue of the estate, and little Roy was to receive $30,000. Anna would also receive a sum of $10,000.

Investigator Morris then asked if he had cohabited with Anna. William Parsons replied, "Absolutely no."

He was then asked if he could afford to pay a ransom in case his wife was kidnapped. William replied, "No, but I have relatives who I believe would help me out if necessary." When asked which family member in particular would help him, William replied, "Mr. Richardson Pratt," the husband of his sister Laura.

William also provided an explanation as to why he wanted to take the train to Huntington that evening rather than get off at the Saint James Station. He claimed that he wanted to get off at Huntington and drive to his home in Stony Brook because the train ride was often rather warm and he liked to have a ride in his automobile before coming home.

After they completed interviewing Anna and William, Investigators Morris and Walker decided to re-search the property immediately surrounding the house. At approximately 1:20 a.m., as Investigator Morris stood by, Investigator Bert Walker began a third search of the Parsonses' Dodge. First, he searched the front area of the car, and finding nothing, he got out of the vehicle and opened the rear door. He shined a flashlight into the rear area and immediately noticed a white envelope on the floor. Three-quarters of the envelope was visible, and one quarter of it was stuck under the footrest in the back of the car. There was nothing else on the floor of the car except this envelope.

Investigator Walker would later state that the note was left in such a position that it must have been placed in the car after the search by the other officers;

This 1937 Dodge D5 is the same make, model and color of the Parsons family car. *Author's collection.*

The Dodge D5 back seat. Two prior searches by officers with five-cell flashlights reportedly failed to notice a white envelope in plain view on the floor. *Author's collection.*

otherwise, it would have been easily found. Unfortunately, standard crime scene evidence preservation practices, developed by Alphonse Bertillon in 1903, despite having been long established, were not followed by any of the three local law enforcement agencies present at the Parsons farm that evening. Most importantly, the ransom note was not photographed before it was moved, which would have memorialized the position of the envelope and, at the same time, corroborated Investigator Walker's observation.

Handling the envelope in his bare hands, Investigator Walker ripped open the envelope and read part of the note that it contained. Once he realized the importance of the note's contents, he brought the note into the house and showed it to Chief Briggs and the other law enforcement officers present, with the exception of Trooper Sullivan, who was on the telephone at the time. After the completion of Trooper Sullivan's call, Investigator Walker showed him the note. Trooper Sullivan copied the words onto a sheet of paper. He was the only individual to copy the information down word for word. All of these actions were done outside the presence of William and Anna. Investigator Walker ensured that no one else physically handled the ransom note that morning, and he placed it in his left-hand coat pocket, where it remained for several hours.

Shortly after the ransom note was discovered, members of the Parsons and McDonell families began to arrive at the farm. These included William's brother John Parsons and his wife, Catherine "Bunny" Parsons, of Bayside. They were followed by William's brother-in-law Richardson Pratt of Glen Cove and Alice's brother Frank McDonell Jr. from New Jersey.

Assistant District Attorney Joseph Arata joined his colleague Harry Brenner at the Parsons farm during the early morning hours. Arata also interviewed Anna Kupryanova. In this interview, she indicated that "Mr. and Mrs. Parsons never quarreled with each other and that they were a happy couple." She added that she was "last married in 1920 and her husband died in an automobile accident on April 24, 1923."

Anna Kupryanova also stated that the garbage man "Cox" came to collect the garbage. Assistant District Attorney Arata asked her directly, "Did you and Mrs. Parsons talk with him?" Anna answered, "Yes, he came in the kitchen and took the things. We gave him feathers. We plucked the squabs and put the feathers in the box and put [it] outside for him."

At some point during the early morning hours, Assistant District Attorney Harry Brenner requested that Investigators Walker and Kehlenbach travel to the Babylon Town Police Station to pick up Assistant District Attorney Lindsay Henry. Bert Walker would later state that there were no reporters

Will Parson i have your wife for 25.000 ransom i calculate you coud get that money in 24 hours. I have no place to keep her longer Meet Bus Terminal in Jamaica pm nine oclock Bring money in Box my man will call you By name and you go with him he will take you to your wife But mind if any cop aBoard you'll pay for it and she will never speak again,

DECLASSIFIED
Authority NND 998212

The original ransom note found after the third police search of the Parsonses' Dodge. *Author's collection.*

at the farm when he and Kehlenbach left to pick up Henry, but many were present when he returned with the attorney.

At approximately 2:30 a.m., the phone rang at the Parsons home. John Harding of the Brookhaven Police Department answered the call. It was the City Desk of the *New York Daily News* and reporters were inquiring as to whether a kidnapping had occurred. Harding denied that there was a kidnapping but did confirm that Alice Parsons was missing.

Twenty minutes later, Norma Abrams, a reporter for the *New York Daily News*, picked up her telephone and called Rhea Whitley at his home. Whitley was the special agent-in-charge (SAC) for the New York office of the Federal Bureau of Investigation. Abrams told SAC Whitley that the *Daily News* had just received information that a woman had been kidnapped in Stony Brook, Long Island, and a ransom note had been found demanding payment of $25,000 for the woman's return. She further stated that the woman in question was Alice Parsons, wife of William H. Parsons of Stony Brook, Long Island, and that she had disappeared at approximately 11:00 a.m. the previous day. She also stated that it was her information that the New York State Police were leading the investigation. Abrams informed SAC Whitley that she had no other details and that she was leaving for Stony Brook immediately.

Shockingly, the ransom note containing the ransom amount of $25,000 had been discovered only *one hour and thirty-five minutes* prior to Abrams's call to SAC Whitley at his home. It must also be noted that there were no reporters present on the farm at this point in the investigation. In addition, neither William nor Anna had been informed of the existence of the ransom note. This indicated that the individual who provided the details of the ransom note to the press had to be one of the eight law enforcement officers present at Long Meadow Farm. It was also abundantly clear that the press now knew exactly where and when the ransom was to be paid.

New York Daily News reporter Norma Abrams would later tell SAC Whitley that the ransom note details, which were later quoted in the newspaper, were obtained from the New York State Police. She indicated that the contents of the note were generally known on the morning of June 10, 1937 by all those gathered at the Parsons farm. The paper carried most of the detailed wording of the ransom note that day, with a verbatim version of the ransom note following in a later edition. In a later conversation with Assistant District Attorney Lindsay Henry, Whitley would learn that New York State Trooper Sullivan sold the contents of the ransom note to a reporter for the sum of $100.

After receiving the initial call from the *Daily News* reporter, SAC Whitley contacted the New York State Police barracks in Bay Shore, Long Island, located approximately fifteen miles from Stony Brook. Whitley talked with the duty sergeant, who confirmed the information that Whitley had received from Norma Abrams. However, the sergeant would not supply any additional information over the telephone. SAC Whitley then dialed the number for Assistant FBI Director Edward A. Tamm in Washington, D.C.

After speaking with Tamm, Whitley contacted his assistant special agent-in-charge (ASAC), T.J. Donegan, and instructed him to proceed to Stony Brook. Donegan was told to bring five special agents with him.

It was now 4:00 a.m., and William Parsons again found himself at his kitchen table being interviewed by John Harding of the Brookhaven Town Police. When Harding asked William if Anna could be harboring feelings of love and affection toward him, he replied, "Well, to be truthful with you, my wife has remonstrated with me about Anna. She said Anna always seems to favor me."

Chief Assistant District Attorney Lindsay Henry arrived at the Parsons farm at 4:45 a.m. He would later state that he had first heard about the incident at about 11:00 p.m. the previous evening and sent a telegram to the FBI's New York office. That message arrived at approximately 5:00 a.m. on June 10.

Alice's brother Frank McDonell lived in Radburn, New Jersey. He

Alice's brother Frank McDonell Jr. arrived at the farm immediately after Alice's disappearance and stayed deeply involved with the investigation for several years. *Courtesy of Three Village Historical Society.*

was vice president of the Dontomatic Corporation of Elizabeth, New Jersey. He had received a long-distance telephone call from William Parsons at about 10:30 p.m. the previous evening. William asked Frank if he had seen Alice that day and advised him of the fact that she appeared to be missing. After they hung up, Frank decided to call back, and he spoke with Lieutenant Stacey Wilson. Wilson suggested that Frank come to Stony Brook immediately.

When he arrived several hours later, he was kept in the driveway area and interviewed by Brookhaven Town Police personnel regarding the home life of his sister, Alice. After about an hour of talking with the police, he entered his sister's home and found William Parsons; William's brother John; John's wife, Bunny; and William's brother-in-law Richardson Pratt in the living room. They all greeted one another and sat down to talk about Alice's disappearance.

Frank recalled that the last time he had been in that house was the previous summer, when one of his children had been there for a visit. It was common for his two children to visit Long Meadow Farm and their aunt Alice for two weeks each summer. One of the things that Frank noticed immediately was the number of police officers inside the house. He counted at least eight or nine in addition to the two assistant district attorneys.

After about an hour, Frank decided to go to his car so that he could think quietly about the situation. A short time later, he was joined by Chief Assistant District Attorney Lindsay Henry, who questioned him about the possible existence of a love triangle between William, Alice and Anna. Frank advised Henry that as far as he knew, his sister and William had a happy home life together. Both men then reentered the house, and Henry went upstairs to conduct an interview. Sometime later, Anna came down the stairs weeping and in a high state of anxiety. Apparently, her feelings had been injured by the type and tone of the questions Henry asked. Bunny Parsons, William's sister-in-law, began to upbraid Lindsay Henry for not acting like a gentleman toward Anna.

Frank McDonell noted later that he felt Henry was more interested in finding motives than he was in finding facts. As it turned out, Lindsay Henry's initial focus on determining a motive behind this crime was undoubtedly the correct course of action to take.

Just before sunrise, Lieutenant Stacey Wilson advised William and Anna that a ransom note had been found. A few minutes later, Frank McDonell was sitting in the living room when Lindsay Henry came up to him and whispered in his ear, "We found a note. The kidnappers want $25,000." This brought a feeling of relief to Frank because he now knew what happened to his sister. He decided to telephone his brother, Howard, in Hollywood, California, to inform him of the situation. Due to all of the commotion and confusion in the house, he decided it would be best if he used a telephone in the village.

6
THE FBI TAKES OVER

On June 10, 1937, at 5:45 a.m., ASAC Donegan, together with Special Agents J.A. Murphy, S.E. Dennis, G.H. Meyer, J.W. Ransom and H.A. Martin, left the New York City field office in two automobiles. They traveled quickly and arrived at Long Meadow Farm on Gould Road at approximately 6:55 a.m.

Just prior to leaving the New York office, ASAC Donegan received a telegram from Lindsay Henry of the Suffolk County District Attorney's Office advising him that there had been a kidnapping at Stony Brook. Lindsay Henry specifically requested that someone from the FBI contact him. Donegan reached Henry by telephone and told him that he was on his way to Stony Brook. Henry provided Donegan with a meeting place in Smithtown and stated that he would have one of his investigators meet him there and then bring him to the farm.

Upon reaching Long Meadow Farm early that morning, ASAC Donegan and Special Agent J.A. Murphy were introduced to Lindsay Henry. Lindsay Henry indicated that he was in charge of the investigation for the District Attorney's Office. They were also introduced to Chief of Police Bridges of the Brookhaven Police Department, Inspector Nugent of the New York State Police and a number of investigators attached to the District Attorney's Office. Henry briefly went over the facts of the case, and Investigator Walker showed the federal agents the ransom note that he had found in the Dodge. He stated that he was the only person to handle the note after it was found.

ASAC Donegan and his team of federal agents immediately began their much-practiced tasks. Special Agent J.W. Ransom contacted the telephone company and made arrangements to have a direct phone line put into the Parsons home. The post office was contacted and arrangements made to have all of the Parsonses' mail held until each letter could be screened and examined by an FBI agent. Equipment was installed that would allow the agents the ability to monitor all incoming and outgoing telephone calls from the Parsonses' telephone number, Stony Brook 359. As these arrangements were taking place, Special Agents G.H. Meyer and H.A. Martin began a thorough examination of the interior of the farmhouse and surrounding grounds. At the conclusion of this examination, Special Agent H.A. Martin interviewed Anna Kupryanova in the upstairs bedroom normally occupied by her son. This was Anna's fifth interview since the arrival of the police at the farm the previous evening.

Anna repeated the events surrounding the prior day's disappearance of Alice Parsons as she had done for Lieutenant Wilson, Chief Briggs, Brookhaven's Officer Harding, District Attorney Investigator Morris and Assistant District Attorney Henry. In this interview, Anna claimed to be the daughter of a member of the Russian nobility of the czar's regime. She claimed that she and her husband left Russia in 1919 due to the revolution and went to London. She stated that her husband died in London in 1926. During her stay in London, her son, Roy, was born. During this interview, she again claimed that Alice and William never quarreled. She also claimed that Alice had inherited $150,000 to $200,000 in property from the late Colonel Timothy S. Williams and added that Alice had already received $25,000 as per the will of Colonel Williams.

During this interview, Special Agent Martin asked Anna to describe the man and woman who had driven away with Alice Parsons in the black sedan. As Anna had informed Lieutenant Stacey Wilson the previous evening, she could not provide a physical description of the man or the woman. She did state, however, that she believed the man was wearing a sailor-type straw hat. She could provide no information about the color or type of license plate on the black car. She stated that Alice parked the Parsonses' car to the rear of the house upon her return from the train station, and it had not been moved. When questioned regarding her relationship with William Parsons, she again claimed that there had never been any improper relations between them and that the home life of the entire family was very pleasant.

Special Agent Martin would later note in his report that due to the numerous interruptions during the interview by local and state police officers, it became too difficult to continue. It was at that point that he deemed it advisable not to continue the interview, and therefore no further inquiries were made of Anna Kupryanova at that time.

As Anna was being interviewed by Special Agent Martin, William Parsons was being interviewed by Special Agent Murphy. During this interview, William discussed the recent changes he and Alice had made to their wills. He stated that the new wills were created due to the fact that Howard McDonell and his wife were expecting a child shortly and he and Alice wanted to include that child in their wills, as they had with Frank McDonell's children. William also discussed his current financial status, including information regarding his mortgage.

ASAC Donegan requested that the ransom note be turned over to him so that he could forward it to the FBI's technical laboratory in Washington, D.C. Lindsay Henry saw no issue with this and ordered Investigator Walker to hand over the ransom note to ASAC Donegan. The ransom note was then given to Special Agent J.D. Milensky, who was charged with personally transporting the note to the FBI's laboratory in Washington.

Once that important piece of physical evidence was secured, ASAC Donegan turned his attention to Alice's brother Frank. Frank McDonell indicated that his sister had been in the best of spirits and that he could not understand why someone would kidnap her. He told Donegan that she had inherited some money, but it was not a large sum and there was no apparent reason for the Parsons family to be marked as being capable of paying a ransom of $25,000.

As the morning unfolded at the Long Meadow farmhouse, the scene became one of complete chaos. William Parsons would later note in his diary, "A mad house of local police. Finally brought under control by putting G men in control. Sent the dogs to board at Dr. Nelson." There were now four separate law enforcement agencies present, representing the local, county, state and federal governments. Each felt they needed to conduct their own investigation, which resulted in what is known in law enforcement as the "silo effect." It basically refers to the lack of information flowing between the investigative agencies. Each agency wanted to hold on to every new nugget of uncovered information in hopes of developing the lead that would solve the case. It also caused the repetition of numerous investigative steps that would have been better served by a singular coordinated effort. These types of issues were common in cases such as this and were immediately recognized by the FBI as a problem that needed to be fixed.

At approximately 9:00 a.m. that morning, ASAC Donegan held a conference with William Parsons, Frank McDonell and Alice's brother-in-law Richardson Pratt. The conference was held on the farmhouse lawn and away from the burgeoning chaos. One observer noted at the time that the house was teeming with law enforcement officials coming and going and that complete confusion reigned. ASAC Donegan began the conversation with these three family members by explaining the FBI's jurisdiction and the fact that the FBI was primarily concerned with the safe return of Alice Parsons and secondarily interested in the apprehension of the criminals.

As ASAC Donegan explained to the family members, the FBI's jurisdiction was based on the Federal Kidnapping Act, popularly known as the Lindbergh Law. The theory behind the Lindbergh Law was that federal law enforcement intervention was necessary due to the fact that state and local law enforcement officers could not effectively pursue kidnappers across state lines. In addition, state and local law enforcement were normally less effective at following investigative leads that took them outside of their individual jurisdictions.

ASAC Donegan then showed each of the individuals the ransom note. Frank McDonell took several notes as to the kidnapper's demands. It was then agreed by all three family members that the FBI would have complete charge of the investigation and that they would cooperate in every possible way. At this point, William Parsons issued a request to have all the other law enforcement officials be immediately withdrawn from his residence. Donegan indicated that he would try. William also stated that he would provide a room in the farmhouse for the exclusive use of the FBI agents. Donegan then informed William that they would be installing a dedicated telephone line in the house.

As the conversation on the lawn continued, Richardson Pratt stated that he would arrange to obtain the $25,000 cash ransom through the Brooklyn Trust Company. Pratt agreed to have an FBI agent accompany him to make a listing of the bills' serial numbers. All three family members agreed that the ransom would be paid to the kidnappers in order to secure Alice's safe return. Pratt stated that he could have the money at his home in Glen Cove by 6:00 p.m. so that William could pick up the money and deliver it to the kidnappers at the Jamaica Bus Terminal at 9:00 pm.

Later that day, it was reported to FBI director J. Edgar Hoover that William S. Alspach, assistant cashier for the Charles Pratt Company in New York City, had delivered 2,500 ten-dollar bills to Richardson Pratt and the FBI. The packages of bills had been phototactically copied. The copies

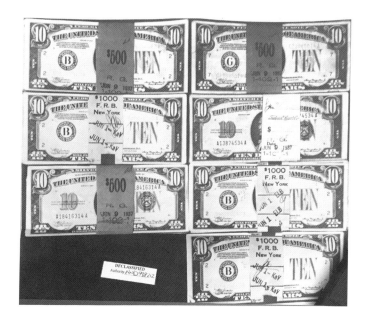

Top: The ransom cash as provided by William Parsons's brother-in-law Richardson Pratt. Each sheet of bills was photographed and serial numbers recorded by the FBI. *From the National Archives.*

Left: These silver certificates were included in the ransom money that was never paid. *From the National Archives.*

comprised three sheets made of thirty packages of bills, with information regarding each packet written on the package's bands. The bills were issued by Federal Reserve Banks from various parts of the country and included silver certificates issued by the treasurer of the United States. The ransom payment for the release of Alice Parsons was now ready to go.

Unfortunately, the immediate need for the ransom money diminished as the day progressed. It was now clear to the FBI that the release of the details of the ransom note to the press precluded any attempt to make a ransom payment at the place and time indicated in the note. Any such attempt would be met by a horde of reporters and photographers, which would undoubtedly scare off any suspect who showed up to collect the ransom. It was decided that the cash would be kept readily available by Pratt and that the FBI would wait for the next communication from the kidnappers.

As ASAC Donegan was holding his conference on the lawn outside the Parsons farmhouse, SAC Whitley of the New York field office was preparing to join his staff in Stony Brook. SAC Whitley, along with Special Agents R.E.A. Boyle, H.G. Robinson, J.E. Seykora, J.R. O'Hair, G.A Callahan and F.I. McGarraghy, loaded technical equipment and weapons into their vehicles and headed for Long Meadow Farm.

Special Agent Meyers was tasked with dealing with the potential evidence that was now lying, uncovered, on the floor of Chief Bridges's personal car. The two axes, seized earlier in the morning by Chief Bridges, needed to be examined for the presence of human blood and hair. Special Agent Meyers, in the presence of Trooper Kaperas, carved an X for identification purposes into the handle of each axe. Assistant District Attorney Henry insisted that the scientific analysis be done immediately and locally. In an incredible waste of investigative manpower, it was decided that four individuals would transport the two evidentiary items to the New York State Hospital for the Insane in Central Islip, which was located just thirteen miles away. Special Agent Meyer, Trooper Kaperas, Investigator Morris and Lieutenant Stacey Wilson all accompanied the evidence to the office of Dr. Trygstadt at the hospital. Although Dr. Trygstadt could easily identify the blood on the axes as being from a chicken, he stated he was not qualified to conduct an analysis of what appeared to be hair on the axe head. A simple microscopic analysis indicated that the blood cells were oval in nature and contained a small nucleus, whereas human cells are round. Dr. Trygstadt recommended that all of the evidence be further examined by Dr. Goettler of Bellevue Hospital in New York City.

The blood and hair evidence was then taken to Bellevue Hospital by Trooper Kaperas. He was met at the hospital by Special Agent O'Donnell and Dr. Goettler. After a short analysis, Dr. Goettler determined that the blood on the axe was chicken blood and the hair was from a dog. He also identified some of the fibers as chicken feathers.

As the blood and hair evidence was being transported into New York City, another major development in the investigation arose. Assistant District Attorney Joseph Arata received information that Leona O. Newton of Stony Brook had seen Alice Parsons at 12:45 p.m. the previous day. This would be approximately one and a half hours after she reportedly left Long Meadow Farm in the black sedan.

Arata briefly interviewed Mrs. Newton at her Main Street home and then brought her directly to the Parsons farm, where she was again interviewed by Lindsay Henry and Special Agent J.A. Murphy. The entire conversation was taken down by stenographer Lloyd Record.

Mrs. Newton stated that she had been a resident of Stony Brook for her entire life and had known Alice Parsons and her family for many years. Mrs. Newton indicated that she had served as the Stony Brook postmistress for several years and would frequently see members of the Parsons family at the post office.

Mrs. Newton stated that on June 9, she listened to radio station WEAF during her lunch, as she did every day. At approximately 12:45 p.m., she put on her hat and picked up two letters that contained news items she had written for the *Port Jefferson Times* and the *County Review* at Riverhead and then turned off the radio. She stated she then went out her front door and walked to her Chevrolet sedan, which was parked in front of her house.

As she was entering her car from the right side, she looked out the left front window and saw an automobile just opposite her car, proceeding in an easterly direction on Main Street at about twenty miles per hour. As she looked at the car, she noticed that Alice Parsons was driving the automobile. Mrs. Newton was not sure if Alice Parsons was alone in the car. She stated that as she was settling herself in the driver's seat, she paused a moment in order to wave her hand in a friendly gesture to Mrs. Parsons as she went by. She said that Mrs. Parsons kept looking straight ahead and apparently did not see her. After Alice Parsons passed Mrs. Newton, Mrs. Newton started her car and did a U turn on Main Street. She was now traveling in the same direction that Alice Parsons had been traveling. Mrs. Newton then turned onto Christian Avenue, and at the corner of Christian and Cedar Avenue, she saw Mr. T.B. Minuse driving his green Hudson sedan. She waved to Mr. Minuse. Mrs. Newton's brief encounter with Mr. Minuse on the corner of Christian and Cedar Avenues was later corroborated by him.

Mrs. Newton described the car that Alice Parsons was driving as steel gray in color. There was no doubt in her mind that the person she had seen the day before was Alice Parsons. However, there was a clear discrepancy as to the color of the car. After Mrs. Newton gave her statement, she was taken outside and asked to review the multiple cars parked in the driveway and surrounding area. She was asked if any of the automobiles resembled the one she had seen Alice driving the day before. Mrs. Newton pointed to the 1937 tan Dodge that belonged to Alice Parsons. She then stated that the reason she had originally believed the vehicle she saw was steel gray was due to the fact that the car previously owned by the Parsons was steel gray in color. She also stated that she was unaware that they had purchased a new automobile.

Assistant District Attorney Lindsay Henry saw this as an opportunity to directly challenge Anna Kupryanova's previous statement that Alice Parsons's car had not been moved since she returned from the St. James railroad station the day before. After Mrs. Newton identified the vehicle that Alice had been driving on Main Street, Henry requested that Anna be brought into the room. This would be just one of the many times this confrontational technique would be used during the course of this investigation. The information supplied by Mrs. Newton was repeated for Anna, and Henry asked Anna to offer an explanation. Anna responded by stating that Alice Parsons had a double in Stony Brook. She then stated that Mrs. Newton probably saw Alice on Tuesday, June 8, because Alice had been to the Three Village Tea Room that day. Lindsay Henry then asked that William Parsons be brought into the room. William was asked if he was aware that Alice had a double in Stony Brook. He indicated that he had never heard that fact before.

SAC Whitley and his agents approached the Parsons farm at approximately 11:45 a.m. His initial observation was that the residence, the grounds surrounding the residence and the road in front of the residence were completely overrun with state police, township police, district attorney personnel, representatives of the press and curiosity seekers. It was clear to SAC Whitley that no organization or system was in place, and it was extremely difficult to find any member of the Parsons family or any individual who might have up-to-date information regarding the investigation.

Within forty-five minutes of his arrival at Long Meadow Farm, SAC Whitley was advised by one of his special agents that the detailed contents of the ransom note had been leaked to the press. After receiving a briefing from ASAC Donegan, SAC Whitley drove into Stony Brook village and telephoned Director J. Edgar Hoover. Whitley advised Hoover of the current developments in the investigation. Whitley mentioned that it had struck him as quite odd that a real kidnapper, who was out for profit, would place the ransom note in such an obscure location as the floor of an automobile. Whitley also made it clear to the director that the current situation at the farm made any intelligent investigative efforts impossible. Director Hoover suggested that it might be advisable for William Parsons to issue a public statement requesting that the farm be cleared of all persons except the Parsons family in order that the way be opened for any contacts from the kidnappers. Hoover also advised Whitley that Inspector E.J. Connelley, who had just completed his trial testimony for a case in Newark, New Jersey, was on his way to Stony Brook and that he would be taking charge of the investigation.

Upon SAC Whitley's return to the farm, he met with both William Parsons and Frank McDonell. Whitley passed on the FBI director's suggestion that Alice's family issue a public statement in an attempt to have the farm cleared of law enforcement, press and bystanders. Both William and Frank agreed to do this and retreated to William's office in the farmhouse. Together they drafted an announcement and spread the word that a public statement from the family was forthcoming.

At approximately 5:00 p.m. on June 10, Inspector Connelley and Special Agent Malone arrived at Long Meadow Farm. Forty-five-year-old Inspector Connelley was considered one of the top FBI men of his time. He had served in the First World War as a lieutenant in the army and studied both law and accounting in New York. He eventually joined the FBI in 1920. He was soon promoted to special agent and served in that capacity in St. Louis, New York, Chicago and Cincinnati. As both an inspector and a SAC, he had worked on many of the FBI's most prominent kidnapping and gangster-related cases of the time. He was clearly a favorite of J. Edgar Hoover.

In a later memorandum to Director Hoover, Inspector Connelley noted that upon his arrival, he observed that Long Meadow Farm was swarming with police, DA personnel and the press. He also noted that the roads surrounding the farm were practically impassable due to all of the vehicles belonging to the multitude of official persons and visitors.

One of Inspector Connelley's first tasks upon arrival was to confirm the agreement that SAC Whitley had reached with the other law enforcement agencies. SAC Whitley had held a meeting with Suffolk County DA L. Baron Hill, Chief ADA Henry, Chief Edward Bridges and Inspector Harold Nugent. During

Inspector E.J. Connelley was one of Director J. Edgar Hoover's top investigators. *Author's collection.*

that meeting, Lindsay Henry, speaking for District Attorney Hill, suggested that the FBI take complete charge of the investigation and that all activities of the interested law enforcement agencies should be coordinated through the bureau. Henry also stated that he would personally put his services and the services of the investigators attached to the DA's office at the FBI's disposal. SAC Whitley responded by saying that the bureau would accept the responsibility of being the lead agency, provided that the other interested agencies were agreeable. Both Chief Bridges and Inspector Nugent agreed to the proposal made by Lindsay Henry.

After Inspector Connelley received a briefing from SAC Whitley, he conferred with William Parsons and Frank McDonell. A short time later, William Parsons released the following typewritten statement to the press:

Because of the tragic events which have occurred, I want to seek the cooperation of the law-enforcement agencies and the newspaper representatives in effecting the safe return of my wife. Due to the unfortunate publicity concerning instructions of the kidnaper, it will of course be impracticable to and useless to attempt to follow the instructions already given by the kidnaper.

However, I want to assure the party or parties holding my wife that I am willing and anxious to follow implicitly and without question any further instructions given and that they will be treated in strictest confidence.

In order that the persons holding my wife for ransom may reach me freely an at any time and without any danger of being observe or overheard, I request that all law-enforcement officials and press representatives withdraw from my residence, the grounds, and the vicinity, so that the coast will be entirely clear to reach me without any risk or danger of observation.

I am sure that the first and foremost concern of all officials and persons interested in the case is the safe return of my wife and I feel sure that everyone will cooperate with me to the fullest extent.

It is my desire to cooperate with the press as far as possible but I am sure that you can understand my reluctance to make any further statements at this time which might in any way jeopardize my wife's safety. I feel certain that the officials and the press will assist me and I again want to assure any party desiring to get in touch with me that all means of communication are open and that I will comply with any demands made.

Immediately following the issuance of the public statement, all fifteen FBI agents and supervisors withdrew from the farm and proceeded to their newly established headquarters just two miles away. The FBI, with its vast resources of manpower and money, had quickly established a footprint in the nearby village of Stony Brook. An entire two-story house was rented on Main Street. The house, known as the Lake View Cottage, was a building with five rooms upstairs for the agents' use; two rooms downstairs to be used as bedrooms; one room to be used as a conference room; one room as an office and one room as a teletype room. There was also a downstairs reception room equipped with a telephone for use by the local law enforcement officials. There were also several separate rooms occupied by the building's owner, a Mrs. Vreeland.

Earlier that day, it had become apparent that the supposedly unlisted numbers of the private telephone installed at the Parsons home and the two lines installed at the Lake View Cottage had become public property. The telephone company was asked to immediately issue new numbers to both locations and was given express instructions not to release those numbers to anyone other than FBI personnel. As an indication of the fragility of the hours-old relationship between the local and federal law enforcement agencies, the FBI requested that the telephone company check the new lines for wiretaps. The very next day, the FBI amended its request to the telephone company and now wanted the telephone lines checked for wiretaps twice each day.

The public visual of the FBI agents leaving the Parsons farm spurred the other law enforcement agencies and the press to do the same. However, the other three law enforcement agencies were unaware of the fact that an agreement had been reached between the FBI and William Parsons that would allow two FBI agents to surreptitiously reenter the house under the cover of darkness. At 11:00 p.m. that evening, Special Agents Boyle and Dennis approached Long Meadow Farm on foot. Once they were convinced that they would not be detected by local law enforcement or the press, they entered the Parsons home.

7

WAR AMONG THE INVESTIGATORS

On June 11, 1937, at approximately 6:00 a.m., the wiretap on the Parsonses' home phone became active. All conversations, incoming and outgoing, from the Stony Brook 359 telephone number would now be monitored from a second-floor bedroom at the FBI's new headquarters on Main Street in Stony Brook.

Later that morning, Inspector Connelley and SAC Whitley noted that the vast numbers of reporters and others at the farmhouse precluded them from conducting proper interviews of William Parsons and Anna Kupryanova. Part of the reason for the sudden surge in the news media presence was that morning's *New York Daily News* headline: "Ransom Waits for Kidnaper."

Inspector Connelley finally decided that it would be best to interview William and Anna at a location that would ensure privacy. He chose the Sammis estate in Huntington. It is important to note that at this point William and Anna had been interviewed by Lieutenant Wilson, Chief Briggs, Brookhaven's Officer Harding, District Attorney Investigator Morris, Assistant District Attorney Arata, Assistant District Attorney Henry and Special Agent H.A Martin. The upcoming interviews with Inspector Connelley would be William's and Anna's eighth in less than twenty-four hours.

The facts as related by William Parsons did not vary greatly from those given during the previous interviews. In this interview, he recounted his movements and actions of the previous day. William did, however, state that that his trips to New York City were "very infrequent." He also claimed,

This *New York Daily News* front page was similar to others in Chicago; Washington, D.C.; and San Francisco. It was a crime story that captivated the entire country. *Photo from Newspapers.com.*

for the first time, that the clerk in the newspaper store at the St. James train station struck him as having a peculiar appearance, as if he had been up all night. He also added that he had seen two or three other men in the store who looked like they had been up all night drinking. William described the newspaper store as being on the left-hand side of the main street. He stated that he had parked the car in front of this store and that when the train pulled into the station he got out of the car and boarded the train. He told Inspector Connelley that that was the last time he had seen his wife, Alice. During the interview, William spoke of his squab business and he advised the inspector that they had achieved few results with the business and had been considering dropping it completely.

Anna Kupryanova was interviewed next. She supplied Inspector Connelley with detailed information regarding her background. This included her maiden name, Shishoff, and the fact that she was born in Crimea. She said that she and Roy had been living in Yugoslavia with her husband. She said that her husband, Alexander Kupryanova, had left Yugoslavia to come to

America. She said she last saw her husband in 1926 and had not seen him since she came to the United States. She stated that she had heard that her husband was in Cleveland and that he was a civil engineer.

As to the events surrounding the disappearance of Alice Parsons, Anna now recalled that the license plate on the car that Alice left in was a New York plate. She stated that she could not see the man very well from the kitchen but noted he was wearing a soft hat. The woman had on a black straw hat with a straight brim.

Inspector Connelley's interviews of William and Anna at the Sammis estate were not extensive. There was still a great deal of background information and many previous statements that needed to be thoroughly analyzed before the appropriate questions could be formalized. William and Anna were soon returned to their farmhouse, where they joined the secreted Agents Boyle and Dennis.

In a memo written by Director Hoover to Assistant Director Tamm, Hoover summarized the day's events in Stony Brook and included the impressions relayed to him by Inspector Connelley. Director Hoover's written summary of his conversation with Connelley included the lines: "Mr. Parsons is a weak sister and it is difficult to get much out of him and that the woman is very crafty." Connelly further observed: "The business appeared to be a hobby of a man who was living on his wife's money." He also stated that the state police were somewhat antagonistic and had not withdrawn from the Parsons property as requested and that they were in fact searching the cisterns in the vicinity. In the memo, Director Hoover expressed his concerns about the security of the FBI phone lines and directed Connelley to continue to ensure that the lines were not tapped. Director Hoover's final comment to his assistant was regarding Connelley's confidence that the bureau was in complete charge of the situation and that with two agents inside the house, nothing could happen without the FBI's knowledge.

The very next day, an incident occurred that would fracture the agreement of cooperation that had been reached by the four law enforcement agencies. The egregious nature of the incident induced a level of suspicion and mistrust between the local and federal law enforcement agencies that would prevail throughout the course of the investigation.

It was the afternoon of June 11, 1937. Inspector Connelley was working at the Stony Brook FBI headquarters. He had just finished reviewing the FBI technical laboratory's findings regarding the ransom note. The report stated that the ransom note and envelope had been examined and that three latent fingerprints had been found. The fingerprints were from a right thumb and right index and left index fingers. Unfortunately, all three of the fingerprints belonged to District Attorney Investigator Bertram Walker, the discoverer of the ransom note.

The laboratory had found the white envelope that had contained the ransom note to be nondescript. However, the ransom note itself provided a great deal of information. The laboratory reported that the note had been hand-printed in pencil on a piece of 5.5-by-9-inch unruled white paper and further advised that a portion of the upper edge of the paper was missing. The technicians believed that this was due to the way it may have been torn from its original pad. The laboratory report then noted what would later become a crucial piece of forensic evidence in the case. The evidence was in the form of a partial watermark, "Cron," under which was the letter "U." This was further identified as the watermark of "Chronicon U.S.A.," which was found only in paper manufactured by the Hammermill Paper Company of Erie, Pennsylvania. Further investigation showed that this particular paper was distributed to only ten Woolworths Stores on Long Island. One of those stores, located at 21 South Ocean Avenue, Patchogue, was only thirteen miles away from Long Meadow Farm.

Just as Inspector Connelley was finishing reading the laboratory report, State Police Inspector Harold Nugent arrived and immediately conferred with Assistant District Attorney Henry, who was working in the reception area. The information relayed to Henry caused him to immediately leave the building. Later in the evening, Inspector Connelley learned from a newspaper reporter that the state police had taken into custody the supposed husband of Anna Kupryanova. The reporter indicated that the state police planned to bring this individual to the Stony Brook headquarters for questioning, and the journalist wanted a comment from the inspector. Connelley simply refused to comment on the information.

Later that evening, Assistant District Attorney Henry arrived at the Stony Brook FBI headquarters in the company of Trooper Sullivan. Lindsay Henry was quite agitated and began moving from room to room while all the time insisting that he be granted an immediate meeting with Inspector Connelley. It appeared that he, and others, had just visited the Parsons home and he was angered by the fact that they had been refused access to the home by Mr. Parsons. Henry claimed that he would not have been angered by this refusal had he been advised what was going on and what the FBI were doing. Connelley responded by reminding Henry that the family had acted entirely in accordance with the conference they had with Mr. Parsons the day before. He then reminded Henry that he was present for that conference.

Assistant District Attorney Henry then advised Inspector Connelley that the state police were holding a man whose identity and name were unknown to him. In a later memorandum to Director Hoover, Connelley would insist, based on Henry's sudden departure earlier that day with State Police Inspector Nugent, that Henry knew full well who was in custody. In Connelley's mind, it was doubtful that the state police and the press would know if Henry did not.

Henry then indicated that the person they had in custody was a definite suspect or probable kidnapper and that he wanted Anna Kupryanova to see this individual and make an identification at the state police headquarters in Bayshore. Inspector Connelley agreed to help facilitate this request with the Parsons family. However, he made it clear that the FBI was not assuming any responsibility for the actions taken by the local authorities and that there was to be absolutely no publicity regarding this law enforcement action. Inspector Connelley then arranged for SAC Whitley to accompany Henry to the Parsons home.

Anna Kupryanova was picked up from the farmhouse and transported to the headquarters in Bay Shore. Shortly after their arrival, SAC Whitley suspected that the local authorities had an ulterior motive in their demand to have Anna Kupryanova present. He learned that earlier that day, the state police had taken into custody Alexander Kupryanova, the former husband of Anna Kupryanova. He had been arrested in Long Island City based on a tip from a newspaper reporter. Whitley knew, as the local authorities knew, that Anna would readily identify him. It took only a short while for the local authorities' motives to become clear. Anna Kupryanova had been brought to this building by the local authorities so that she could be interrogated. The interrogation lasted for hours, with Anna being shifted from room to room by various state troopers. All during this time, SAC Whitley would catch glimpses of Lindsay Henry and Inspector Nugent. SAC Whitley, representing the lead investigative agency, had no idea who was questioning Anna Kupryanova and what questions were being asked. It became clear to SAC Whitley that the Anna was purposely being moved about in order to obstruct him from knowing what was occurring in the case. In a followup FBI report, SAC Whitley stated:

> When it became apparent that Inspector Nugent and Mr. Henry were deliberately trying to prevent me from being present at the interview of Alexander Kupryanova and his former wife Anna Parsons, formerly Anna Kupryanova, I finally located Inspector Nugent and demanded an explanation of the action being taken. I also insisted that he immediately

inform Assistant District Attorney Henry that I want to see him. Inspector Nugent then went to the room where Mr. Henry was at that time questioning Anna Parsons and her former husband, and brought me to the Inspector's office. There was also present in the Inspector's office Assistant District Attorney Arata. I advised them that I had accompanied Mr. Henry and Trooper Sullivan to the Bay Shore Barrack with Mrs. Anna Parsons for the purpose of being present when she viewed the alleged suspect in the kidnapping; that obviously their real purpose in arranging to bring her to the barracks was to question her generally and intensively regarding the kidnapping and her previous experience and activities; that they also were obviously endeavoring to handle the questing in such a manner that I would not be aware of what was going on, what treatment was being accorded the persons being questioned, or what information, if any, was developed.

At one point during the confrontation between SAC Whitley and Assistant District Attorney Henry, Whitley stated that the local authorities were acting in bad faith and that if they could not work in harmony with the bureau, the bureau would withdraw from the investigation. Then an angry Lindsay Henry accused the bureau of withholding information that was critical to the investigation. Whitley heatedly denied this and informed all present that he would be immediately reaching out to Inspector Connelley.

SAC Whitley left the room to find a telephone to call Inspector Connelly so that he could inform him of the events currently unfolding at the state police barracks. Just after Inspector Connelley finished his conversation with SAC Whitley, his office telephone rang again. This time it was a representative of the telephone company who had called to confidentially inform him that two New York State troopers had requested that he, the telephone company operator, interrupt and disconnect the call that had just been made to the FBI office from the state police headquarters in Bay Shore. The telephone company operator had refused to comply with the state police's request.

After SAC Whitley completed his call to Inspector Connelley, he immediately addressed Assistant District Attorney Henry. He advised him that any questions regarding future cooperation between the agencies in this case would be dealt with by Inspector Connelley upon his arrival. Henry, sensing that the FBI was on the verge of withdrawing completely from the investigation, suddenly took on a more conciliatory tone and offered to have Whitley sit in on the interrogation of Anna. He also offered to have the stenographer read back statements already made by both Anna and Alexander Kupryanova.

It was close to 2:00 a.m. when Inspector Connelley, along with Special Agents Donegan and Meyer, left their Stony Brook headquarters and headed for the state police barracks in Bay Shore. As they pulled up to the barracks, they saw that the place was completely overrun by newspaper reporters and photographers. It was clear that the local authorities had not kept their word, given just hours ago, that there would be no publicity regarding Anna Kupryanova's attempt to identify a suspect in the case. The reporters and photographers literally blocked every entrance to the building.

Inspector Connelley and his agents had to push their way onto the barracks property. Once they managed to make their way to an entrance door, they were met by Inspector Harold Nugent, who had met Connelley earlier that day in Stony Brook but now appeared reluctant to allow the FBI into the building. At Inspector Connelley's insistence, the door was finally opened. Once inside, Connelley and the agents were brought into a room where they met with SAC Whitley, Inspector Nugent, Chief Bridges and Assistant District Attorneys Henry and Arata.

Inspector Connelley began the conversation by directly addressing Henry. He demanded to know what exactly Henry expected to accomplish by taking this course of action. Connelley made it clear to Henry that Henry's answer would be the determining factor in any continued involvement in this case by the FBI. Henry provided no direct answer but instead went into a lengthy discourse regarding the errors in judgment he had committed that evening and followed this with repeated apologies. What was made immediately clear in the mind of Inspector Connelley was that the local law enforcement authorities, after much hype to the press, did not have the kidnapper or murderer in custody and had gathered no new information that would take them any closer to finding Alice Parsons.

Inspector Connelley went on to state to those in the room that if the bureau was to accept responsibility as the lead agency in this investigation, it was not going to be placed into a position that would allow for actions that could jeopardize the safe return of Alice Parsons. He then stated that if they were not agreeable to this, the FBI would immediately withdraw from the investigation and issue a public statement to that effect. Lindsay Henry clearly understood the ramifications of such a public statement and promised full cooperation and disclosure from that point forward. He then requested that the FBI assume full responsibility for the investigation in every detail. Connelly then turned his attention to Chief Bridges and State Police Inspector Nugent and asked them directly if they too were in agreement with Lindsay Henry's assurances and request. Both answered in a "sullen and reluctant manner" that they would comply with whatever conditions were agreed on by Lindsay Henry.

Inspector Connelley had one final point to make and one final important card to play that evening. It was a card that he would successfully use during his future dealings with the local authorities in this case. It had to do with the handling of confidential information. Connelley brought up the issue of the release of the ransom note to the press and how that impeded the investigation and may have jeopardized the life of Alice Parsons. He reminded everyone in the room that the building they were now standing in was surrounded by the press due to the fact that confidential information had been released. These breaches of trust would undoubtedly allow the FBI to justify withholding future case developments from the local authorities. Inspector Connelley stated:

> *I believe that anyone who is responsible for any action as occurred on this night should be held accountable for the consequence of what might occur. It is my opinion that the person who was responsible for disclosing to the newspapers the contents of the first ransom note, should the victim in this case be found dead as a result of such disclosure of the note, would be guilty of the murder of the Alice Parsons.*

Inspector Connelly reminded all those gathered in the room that he had not yet been advised by any of them that Alexander Kupryanova had been arrested. State Police Inspector Nugent, in an effort to minimize their actions, said that the information regarding Alexander Kupryanova's arrest had not been generally known to anyone. It was clearly the wrong thing to say. Connelley quickly reminded Inspector Nugent that the information had actually been generally known to practically every newspaper reporter in the streets of Stony Brook at 7:00 p.m. the previous evening. At the end of the meeting, it was clear that local law enforcement had attempted a gambit and had lost. The consequence of that loss was their now greatly diminished role in the investigation into the kidnapping of Alice Parsons.

Once the conference among the agencies was complete, it was made clear to Connelley that the local authorities were anxious to get Anna Kupryanova off their hands. Connelley arranged for her to be driven home by the FBI. On the ride back to Long Meadow Farm, Anna Kupryanova stated that she had been continually questioned as to who was in the farmhouse. She indicated that she did not reveal the presence of Agents Boyle and Dennis

Anna Kupryanova's former husband, Alexander, as he is being held for questioning by the New York State Police. *Photo courtesy of Three Village Historical Society.*

and did not disclose the fact that she had met with the FBI at the Sammis estate the day before.

It was 3:30 a.m. when Anna stepped into the farmhouse. She and the agents were met at the door by William Parsons and Alice's brother Frank McDonell. A lengthy explanation of what had occurred took place. Inspector Connelley did his best to reassure them that the evening's occurrence would not be repeated.

The next day, June 12, 1937, was Roy Parsons's eleventh birthday. He spent most of the day at the farm with his mother, Anna. He then packed for his upcoming two-day visit to Richardson and Laura Pratt's home in Glen Cove.

It was clear to Inspector Connelley that William Parsons was not holding up well under the stress. The previous night's events involving Anna and the unflattering reports in the newspapers were now taking a toll on him. That same day, the *New York Post* carried the detailed story of Alexander Kupryanova's arrest and his relationship with Anna. Other newspapers reported verbatim questions and answers that appeared to have been taken directly from the transcript of the interrogation. William also learned that day that his sister Laura Pratt had received a threatening letter in the mail; it claimed she was to soon face the same fate as her sister-in-law Alice. This prompted Laura's husband, Richardson Pratt, to surround their Glen Cove home with armed Pinkerton agents.

The information provided during the interrogations of Anna and Alexander Kupryanova at the state police barracks that night did turn out to be of great value to the FBI in assessing Anna's truthfulness and the reliability of the sequence of events as relayed by her. In response to questions asked by Assistant District Attorney Henry, Anna falsely stated that she had lived with Alexander Kupryanova in London for ten months in 1925. She also stated that she had two children with Alexander and that one of them was a little girl born in 1924 who had only lived for about one year. The other child was Roy.

At some point during the course of Anna's interrogation, Lindsay Henry again tried, as he had the day before, the tactic of direct confrontation as a means of shaking the resolute Anna Kupryanova. Anna's former husband, Alexander, was brought into the interrogation room, and Anna's statements were read back to him. These statements included her contention that she had never written a letter to him regarding her unfaithfulness. In response to her statements, Alexander emphatically stated that he had never been in England and that he did receive a letter from Anna in which she said she had been unfaithful, was expecting a child and wanted a divorce. He went on further to state that he had seen Anna and Roy in 1930, when they arrived at Ellis Island in New York. He believed that Roy was approximately three years old at the time. At the end of the confrontation, Anna reiterated her contention that Alexander Kupryanova was Roy's father. Alexander Kupryanova reiterated his statement that he was not the father.

Although no new investigative leads in the disappearance of Alice Parsons were developed that evening, new insights into the enigma that was Anna Kupryanova had begun to emerge.

It was on this day that the FBI began its search for, and review of, the immigration records associated with Anna Kupryanova. Special Agent J.D. Milensky met with Assistant Director Charles P. Muller of the Immigration and Naturalization Service at his office on Washington Street in New York City. Muller informed Agent Milensky that he had been deluged for the past two days with requests from various newspaper men for information regarding Anna Kupryanova. He advised Agent Milensky, in the strictest of confidence, that he had received a telephone call yesterday from his superiors ordering him to immediately send the original file for Anna Kupryanova, alias Anna Cooper, alias Anna Parsons, to Washington, D.C. The original file had been mailed the day before directly to Acting Commissioner of Immigration and Naturalization Edward J. Shaughnessy.

Later that afternoon, several calls were placed to the Parsonses' home telephone. Most of these calls were from reporters and from reporters pretending to be family members. In addition to these calls, the bureau had begun the process of determining which calls and letters might be from the kidnappers and which calls and letters might be from the host of charlatans and extortionists that would continually plague the investigation.

As William Parsons was attempting to deal with the day's events, the little village of Stony Brook had taken on a carnival atmosphere. The population of the village had been swelled by thrill seekers hoping to witness some activity in the search for Allice Parsons. The stores were jammed, and one restaurant was forced to close its door when it ran out of food. Several residents set up hot dog stands and served quick luncheons right from their front porches. Many of the visitors decided to stay for the weekend and took rooms in private homes. All of this led to a constant stream of automobiles that jammed the local roads all day and into the night.

All of these tension-filled activities resulted in a call to the Parsonses' family physician. Later that evening, Dr. Coburn Campbell of Port Jefferson caused a great stir within the press community when he arrived at the Parsonses' farm. Unbeknownst to the press, the purpose of the visit was to administer a sedative to William Parsons.

The next day, June 13, 1937, William Parsons issued a typewritten statement to the press gathered at his home. The statement read:

> *This is the fifth day since the disappearance of my wife Alice. I am worried and distraught. The strain has been very great not knowing whether she is safe and well cared for. We of course are at the mercy of the person or persons responsible for her disappearance. I again wish to assure this person or persons that I stand ready to comply with the instructions they may give. Whatever is humanly possible will be done by me to see that anything they may request will be complied with in secrecy. I request the person or persons to immediately communicate with me in order to expedite the return of Mrs. Parsons.*
>
> *To the press and all law enforcement officers, I have a special request to make. Judging from the wholehearted and sincere efforts of these gentlemen to comply with my prior message to them, I know you will again grant me the favors requested which will be appreciated by a family in their hour of need.*

Due to the possible unthinking actions of certain individuals who have again congested the area about my home, I again request that all such activity about my home of this nature cease and the persons again withdraw. I know that these actions have been sincere efforts of such persons to help or at least to do what they believe is the correct thing; still I cannot but think this has seriously hampered developments to date.

In conclusion, I wish to advise of my sincerity in requesting this and my appreciation of the consideration shown by all persons addressed.

William H. Parsons

Alice's brother Howard McDonell arrived from California on June 15 and immediately met with his brother, Frank, and Richardson Pratt. He was then briefed as to what information had been developed so far in the investigation. He would soon become the voice and face of the family in their efforts to have Alice safely returned.

8
THE SEARCH

One of the key advantages of having Special Agents Boyle and Dennis physically living inside the Parsons home was that it gave them ample opportunity to search the premises. On one afternoon, in the second week of June, they were left alone in the house for a few hours and they methodically continued their efforts to find any scrap of evidence that could assist them in locating Alice Parsons. While searching the upstairs, Agents Boyle and Dennis discovered a pair of stained women's socks believed to belong to Alice. These were packaged and immediately sent to the FBI's laboratory. Later analysis of the stains on the socks indicated the presence of human blood.

Their search of the upstairs also produced three loose sheets of paper found at different locations within Roy's bedroom. Two of the loose sheets were found in Roy's writing desk. The third sheet was found between two pages of the second volume of a book titled *The World War*. The book itself had been on a shelf in Roy's bookcase. The sheet of paper removed from *The World War* book had a hand-drawn sketch of a plane. The sketch, just like the ransom note, contained a watermark that read "Chronicon U.S.A."

A thorough search was also being conducted of all of the outbuildings at Long Meadow Farm. Special Agents Martin and Ward were given specific instructions to conduct a detailed search of the numerous outbuildings on the property. They started with the detached garage, which was also used for the storage of farming equipment.

Above: Roy's airplane drawing, found between the pages of a schoolbook in his room, contained the same watermark as the ransom note. *From the National Archives.*

Left: The ransom note watermark was unique to a writing tablet sold by the Woolworth's store in Patchogue, Long Island. Anna Kupryanova admitted to buying writing paper from that very store. *From the National Archives.*

Every tool, especially those with sharp edges, was examined carefully. Tools with dark stains were immediately subjected to a benzidine test for the presence of blood. Any caked-on material that appeared to be stained was collected for laboratory analysis. The same procedure was followed for any stained work clothes, coveralls, gloves and rags.

Agents Martin and Ward also searched the granary and the pigeon cotes, which were connected to the garage. All three of these structures had cement floors. Just south of the pigeon cotes was another building used for storing packing cans for the squab paste and extra lumber storage. This building also had a cement floor. There was a tool house on the property that held a small tractor, cultivators and hand tools, all of which were examined for possible bloodstains. This building had a cement floor as well. One of the remaining outer structures appeared to be a small museum containing miscellaneous items created by Roy Parsons. There was a collection of tropical shells with a note that stated, "From Aunt Bunny and Uncle John, June 12, 1936." The flooring in this building was made of wood. Each nail in the floor was carefully examined for signs that it might have been removed and then reset. Agents Martin and Ward continued their search within the hen houses and the brooder houses. When those were complete, they turned their attention to the various refuse piles and cisterns that dotted the grounds. Agent Ward had the unpleasant duty of climbing down the eleven feet to the floor of one of the cisterns and carefully examining any material at the bottom.

Agents Martin and Ward located an above-ground cesspool cover on the north side of the Parsons home. The cover had been bolted to a base, and it was apparent from the amount of rust present on the bolt threads that they had not been removed for some time. The agents decided to open it anyway. Unfortunately, their examination of its contents failed to find anything of significance. They also located four additional cesspools that serviced the farmhouse. These were located just south and southwest of the residence. The locations were easily identified by the depressions in the earth that covered each cesspool's lid. Since the earth had not been disturbed, it was decided not to examine each of the cesspool's contents. That decision would be reversed at a later point in the investigation and would result in the discovery of some important corroborating evidence.

While the agents were searching the farmhouse and its surrounding buildings, Inspector Connelley was drawing up plans for an upcoming massive ground search to be conducted in an eight-square-mile area surrounding Long Meadow Farm.

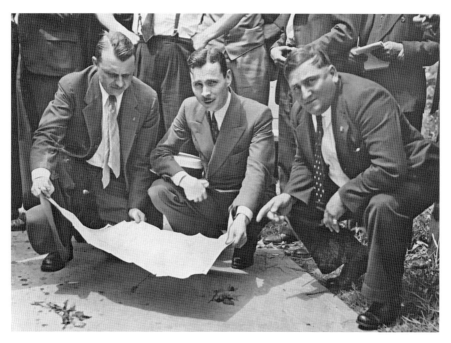

Assistant District Attorney Henry, Inspector Connelley and Chief Bridges reviewing the search map. *Courtesy of Three Village Historical Society.*

On Monday afternoon, June 14, 1937, Inspector E.J Connelley stood in front of the assembled 115 law enforcement officers and volunteer searchers who had gathered inside the Stony Brook Boy's School auditorium. In addition to the officers and volunteers, the state police had brought along their bloodhounds Sappho and Big Red. As Connelley addressed the group, he provided an outline of the search plan and instructions that needed to be followed. This would be the largest and longest ground search ever conducted on Long Island, and it was expected to continue for a minimum of five straight days.

The entire search operation would be led by the FBI's ASAC T.J. Donegan. The search party was divided into five groups, and each group would maintain a team leader. Signal communications were established; two special agents in each group were provided with whistles and compasses. The five groups formed a long line along Gould Road. When the signal was given, they proceeded in unison in an easterly direction. As the groups moved east, they tied cloth strips to trees, indicating that the area had been searched. The area that was covered included cultivated fields and large sections of heavy woodlands. In addition, over twenty miles of roads were covered, with searches extending two hundred feet on each side of the roads.

115 volunteers leaving the Stony Brook Boy's School Auditorium to begin the search for Alice Parsons. *Courtesy of Three Village Historical Society.*

Search team members lined up on the streets in Stony Brook ready to begin their search. *Author's collection.*

Top: The state police bloodhounds Sappho and Big Red were brought in to assist in the search. *Courtesy of Three Village Historical Society.*

Bottom: Searchers checking brush along every roadside within the search area. *Courtesy of Three Village Historical Society.*

Searchers checking old wells and cisterns. *Courtesy of Three Village Historical Society.*

As the search proceeded during the week, the number of volunteers fell off considerably each day. By the third day of the search, the search party was down to about eighty individuals. All during the search, the average state police participation was eight state troopers. The DA's office sent one investigator. On the last day of the search, the Brookhaven Police Department failed to send any officers. Fortunately, Captain Colgan of the Civilian Conservation Corps camp at Huntington provided thirty-five individuals to assist with the search. The eight-square-mile search was completed at 6:00 p.m. on Friday, June 18, 1937.

One unfortunate incident did occur during the search on this last day. Special Agent George H. Treadwell received a severe laceration to his right eye while searching for Alice's remains in a heavily wooded area. In the end, this massive search provided no new information regarding the disappearance of Alice Parsons. However, it was believed that the search was so thorough and complete that it was impossible that her body was anywhere within eight square miles of Long Meadow Farm.

The FBI's search during this time was not limited to Stony Brook and Long Island. There were numerous false sightings in New York City; New London, Connecticut; and other places. Each of these sightings was thoroughly investigated by the bureau. However, Inspector Connelly knew that there was a distinct possibility that Alice Parsons had left the area voluntarily. With that theory in mind, he ordered his agents to thoroughly review the pertinent passenger lists for the Orient Point ferries, Port Jefferson ferries and the steamship lines leaving New York Harbor.

Only one of the two ferry boats at Orient Point was working on June 9 and 10. It was the ferry boat *Steamer Yankee*, then tied up at New London with its crew awaiting their new orders. The FBI dispatched agents, and the crew members were interviewed and shown photographs of Alice Parsons.

Special Agent J.J. Keating conducted the investigation at the Bridgeport and Port Jefferson Steamboat Company. This company, as its name implies, runs daily ferries between Bridgeport, Connecticut, and Port Jefferson, New York. The ferry terminal at Port Jefferson was only 6.6 miles from the Parsons farm. However, on the day of June 9, 1937, the ferry company had only one departure from Port Jefferson Harbor. The ferry boat *Park City* left the Port Jefferson dock at 9:00 a.m. and arrived in Bridgeport one hour and twenty minutes later. Twenty-four employees of the steamboat company were interviewed, with six of the employees stating that they were personally acquainted with Alice Parsons. Unfortunately, no one recalled seeing Alice on that day.

The FBI's New York field office determined that 296 ships had sailed from New York Harbor during the period of inquiry. Of these, 99 carried passengers. A check of the passenger lists for these ships failed to produce any passenger by the name of Alice Parsons.

In an effort to better understand Alice's emotional and mental state prior to her disappearance, Inspector Connelley ordered his agents to interview members of Alice's family. It was the hope that these interviews might shed some light as to the best places to search for Alice Parsons.

One of the first to be interviewed was Frank McDonell. While being questioned by Special Agents Boyle and Dennis, he said that he was convinced from the first that his sister had been kidnapped because of the note that was found and his own observations since his arrival at the farm. He said that after watching William and Anna over a period of several days, he was convinced that there was no improper association between the two. He also stated that while he believed his sister's disappearance was caused by a kidnapping, he felt, as time went on without her return, that her disappearance may have been caused by a "kidnapping gone wrong." He went on to tell the agents that he did not believe his sister was the type of person who would go away of her own free will or that she would become involved with some other man who might influence her disappearance. He also said that he had never known his sister to absent herself from home at any time in the past without a good explanation or reason for it. He also wanted to make it clear that he knew Anna only casually and had met her only a few times prior to Alice's disappearance.

Alice's brother Howard was also interviewed. He had little to offer when it came to Alice's personal habits or her home life. Although they had communicated in letters, he had seen his sister only once in nine years, on the occasion of his wedding in California the previous year. He did say that at the time of her visit she appeared to be healthy, happy and free from any mental disturbance. Howard, like Frank, felt that Alice had been kidnapped and the plans of the kidnappers had gone wrong. He also stated that he did not believe that William or Anna had any connection with Alice's disappearance or that there was any close association between them other that what appeared to be normal by virtue of their positions in the household.

Howard McDonell was also interviewed by Assistant District Attorney Henry. At Henry's request, the meeting was clandestine in nature. Howard was transported by the FBI to a secure location on State Route 25 a few miles from the farm. During the course of the interview, Henry explored the various theories of the case, namely the kidnapping theory, the voluntary disappearance theory and the murder theory.

With reference to the voluntary disappearance theory, Howard McDonell told them that although the arrangement in his sister's home seemed unusual not only to outsiders but also to other members of the family, it apparently had worked out satisfactorily for William and Alice. He stated that as far as he knew, William and Alice had always been very happily married and that all who lived in the household had a congenial relationship. He told Henry that Alice was a friendly, jovial individual who enjoyed the life she led at Long Meadow Farm and that no one in the family had reason to believe that there was any dissatisfaction that might cause his sister to voluntarily disappear. Howard went on to say that had the disappearance been planned by anyone in the household, and carried out with their collusion, the most logical motive for such a move would be defeated because it would be impossible for either William or Anna to receive anything from Alice's estate until a sufficient number of years had elapsed to raise the presumption of her death. Howard then made it clear to Lindsay Henry that William had emphatically told him that there had never been any relations between himself and the Russian woman other than friendly sociability.

Young Roy Parsons was interviewed several times during the days immediately following Alice's disappearance. One of those interviews was conducted by Special Agents Ward and Schroeder in the home of William's sister Laura Pratt in Glen Cove. Roy stated that on June 9, 1937, he had awakened at about 6:00 a.m. This was a half hour earlier than his usual morning wake-up time. He stated that he was up earlier than usual due to William Parsons's trip to New York City and some chores that he had to do before breakfast. He went on to say that all four members of the family sat down to breakfast at about 7:00 a.m. and that William and Alice left for the train station at about 7:35 a.m. After he finished his breakfast, he got on his bicycle and headed for school. He had to make a special stop that morning at Mrs. Melville's Tea House in Stony Brook to water some plants. He believed he left the farmhouse at about 7:45 a.m.

In this interview with the FBI, Roy added a new and critical piece of information that had not been mentioned in his previous statements to local law enforcement authorities. He now added the fact that shortly after he left the farmhouse on his bicycle, he passed Mrs. Parsons on the main road about two hundred feet from the farmhouse. She was heading toward the farm and waved to him as she passed.

Roy went on to say that he was with his friend Harold Kerwin after school for a short while and then went to see his friend Johnny Boshinski. Roy and Johnny then went to hunt for birds' nests. He recalled arriving home sometime around 5:30 p.m. and asking his mother for a peppermint candy. When he asked about the whereabouts of Alice, his mother told him that she had gone to the Sammis place with some people in their car at about 11:15 a.m. and that she was supposed to have come home for lunch but that she had not returned. He stated that his mother seemed curious and worried about Alice's delay. He went on to say that William Parsons returned home at about 6:00 p.m. and immediately began making telephone calls in an attempt to find Alice.

As the four-day ground and sea search for Alice was winding down, with no word from the kidnappers, the family decided that a new press statement should be issued. On June 21, 1937, at 2:45 p.m., the following statement

William Parsons and Frank McDonell conducting a news conference at farm. *Courtesy of Three Village Historical Society.*

was issued by William Parsons to all of the press representatives assembled outside of the farmhouse:

> *I believe all agencies, law enforcement and the press have graciously withdrawn in order that the person holding my wife Alice could in safety reach me. It is now thirteen days since the unhappy calamity of June 9th struck us, a grief stricken family.*
>
> *All members of the family join me in our helpless situation in a plea to the person holding my wife to arrange her safe and immediate return. All our assurances to these persons are again given. We will abide by the wishes of the person who is in position to arrange her return.*
>
> *Due to the lapse of time we must request that the persons concerned immediately furnish to us definite assurance and proof she is alive at this time. Also some definite identification that the person we are dealing with is the person who is holding my wife.*

I therefore urgently request that the person furnish me at once with the proof requested in a further communication and the ways and means by which I may reach you in safety to yourself.

If nothing is heard by noon Thursday, June 24ᵗʰ I will make request to the law enforcement officers to immediately proceed with any possible action to bring to justice the persons responsible for my wife's disappearance.

On this same day, Inspector Connelley forwarded to the FBI's technical laboratory in Washington, D.C., several pages of hand printing for Howard McDonell, Frank McDonell, William Parsons and Roy Parsons. In addition, there were sixteen pages of printing completed by Anna Kupryanova. He requested that the FBI laboratory compare all of these handwriting specimens with the hand printing contained in the original ransom note.

9

THE LIES

When people begin to deny things, then the thing becomes important.
—Inspector E.J. Connelley

One thing was perfectly clear to both local law enforcement and the FBI: The vast majority of the known facts in this case were derived from statements made by William Parsons, Anna Kupryanova and, to some extent, Anna's son, Roy. As the investigation progressed, it became increasingly apparent to Inspector Connelley that the statements of these three individuals contained numerous contradictions. Within two weeks of Alice's disappearance, the FBI began to focus its attention on Anna Kupryanova as the lead suspect, with William Parsons as a possible accomplice.

The FBI's focus on Anna was based on three simple facts. First, two weeks had passed, and there had been no further contact with the kidnappers. This fact was in direct contradiction to the way most other kidnappings progressed. Normally, kidnappers want their ransom immediately and will make every effort to collect their demanded payment. Second, the three sheets of paper found in Roy's bedroom contained the same watermark as the ransom note. Third, both William Parsons and Anna Kupryanova had told numerous lies over the prior two weeks.

However, rather than immediately confronting them on every little lie, as attempted by Assistant District Attorney Henry, Inspector Connelley planned a different strategy—one that he hoped would expose both Anna and William to be the murderers he now believed them to be.

William's lies began just after the arrival of Brookhaven Town Police lieutenant Stacey Wilson on the night of Alice's disappearance. However, Anna Kupryanova's lies began long before she entered the United States in 1930. Her first reported lie was recorded in the immigration files maintained at Ellis Island. It occurred during her first attempt to enter the United States on March 12, 1924. When she arrived at Ellis Island that year, she told the Board of Special Inquiry that she and her husband of five years, Alexander Kuprianova, had three children and all of the children had perished. In reality, Alexander and Anna had only one child, named Melochka, who died within her first year. This was confirmed in Anna's own handwriting in a 1926 letter to Alexander in which she was seeking a divorce.

Anna Kupryanova's second attempt to enter the United States in 1930 required that she file a sworn "Statement of Facts" in filing her Declaration of Intention. In answer to question number 7, Anna stated that she was coming to the United States to join her husband, that the name of her husband was Alexander Kupryanova and that they had one child by the name of Roy Kupryanova. Her final Certificate of Citizenship, #4031568, reads as follows:

Age	*35*
Sex	*Female*
Complexion	*Fair*
Eyes	*Brown*
Hair	*Light Brown*
Height	*5' 8"*
Weight	*160*
Material Status	*Married*

However, she had been divorced from Alexander for five years and Roy was not Alexander's child. The information that Anna supplied for Roy's birth certificate in 1926 indicated that the boy's name was Roy Chandra and the boy's father was Hans Roy Soni, a student of economics. Anna stated in an FBI interview that after the divorce from her husband, she lived with Hans Soni in Kew Gardens, London, and married him six months prior to Roy's birth. She claimed that Soni took her to a Brahmin temple in London, where a religious wedding ceremony by a Brahmin priest was performed and a certificate of marriage was issued to her, written in the Brahmin language. She also claimed that the certificate had been lost. She went on to state that she had been advised by the high commissioner for India that her husband, Soni, together with others, had been killed in an automobile accident somewhere in the south of France and that Soni had been buried there. The much-alive Han Soni would later, in a sworn affidavit, deny that he was the father of Anna's son and would also deny that they were ever married. U.S. State Department inquiries to the English government indicated that there was no record of a marriage between Anna Kupryanova, or Anna Shishoff, and Hans Roy Soni. An inquiry to the high commissioner of India by the American Consul General indicated that that there were no Brahmin temples in London. Similar inquiries to the government of India could find no record of any communication between the high commissioner and Anna Kupryanova.

Anna Kupryanova's much-practiced art of lying to government authorities regarding her personal history continued on the night of Alice's disappearance. One of the first lies Anna told John Harding of the Brookhaven Town Police was that her husband was dead. Then, in the early morning hours of the next day, Anna told Investigator Morris of the District Attorney's Office that her husband had been killed in an automobile accident in Serbia in 1936. Two hours later, Anna was interviewed by Assistant District Attorney Arata. In that interview, she stated that she was last married in 1920 and that her husband was killed in an automobile accident on April 24, 1923. She was again interviewed at the farmhouse just after dawn that same morning, by FBI agent H.A. Martin. In this interview, she claimed that she and her husband left Russia and went to London in 1919. She said her husband lived there with her until his death in 1926.

In reality, her former husband was alive and well, and government records showed that he was never in England. These were just a few of the lies Anna Kupryanova told during the initial hours of the investigation. There were more lies to come, and those lies involved the facts surrounding Alice Parsons's disappearance.

When Lieutenant Stacey Wilson arrived at the Parsons farm on the night of Alice's disappearance, he asked Anna to provide a description of the man and woman who had driven away with Alice in their car. Anna clearly stated that she was unable to provide any description of these individuals. During an interview with Special Agent H.A. Martin a few hours later, Anna then claimed the man driving the car was wearing a sailor-type straw hat. In an interview with Inspector Connelley and SAC Whitley the next day, Anna stated, "The man was wearing a soft hat. The woman had a black straw hat, straight brim, like a man wears. They looked like a middle-aged couple. The woman looked heavy. I never saw the man or woman out of the car. I suppose the woman had dark hair." In a later statement to the press, Anna described the couple in the car: "The woman was round faced and double chinned, tall and heavy set, weighing about two hundred pounds, about forty-five years old, lacking makeup, brown hair pinned smoothly back, wearing a small navy blue hat trimmed with flowers and a blue silk dress of good quality. The man was long faced, with pasty complexion, about thirty-five years old wearing a soft brown hat and a brown suit."

The one thing that was abundantly clear to Inspector Connelley was that Anna Kupryanova had gone from being unable to supply any description of the couple to a rather detailed sketch of the couple as the investigation progressed. It was a vivid picture of two individuals who, Anna claimed, never got out of their car.

One of the key reasons for suspecting Anna Kupryanova in Alice's disappearance was the issue surrounding the Parsonses' Dodge. Anna had claimed, in several different interviews, that Alice parked the car next to the kitchen door at the back of the house when she returned from dropping Bill Parsons off at the train station that morning. She also claimed that the car had not been moved all day and that she could not have moved the car herself because she didn't know how to drive. William Parsons later corroborated her statement to the FBI. The problem for Anna arose when the FBI determined that the Dodge had been moved that morning.

Anna had claimed in an interview with Special Agents Boyle and Dennis that on the morning of June 9 she and Alice were in the kitchen treating an injured gosling when the garbage man arrived to collect the trash. She claimed the refuse was in a big can at the back of the house near the barberry bushes and stated that the trash was always set outside and none of the trash men ever came into the basement for trash. She claimed that she went downstairs to get a big box of feathers and brought those upstairs, and while Alice held the outside door open from the inside, she set the box of feathers down without saying a word. She further stated that she believed the trash pickup occurred at approximately 10:55 a.m. She went on to state that five minutes after the trash man left, the man and woman arrived in the black sedan.

It would later be learned that the information Anna provided in this interview was in direct contradiction to a key witness's statement.

The information that raised Inspector Connelley's suspicions regarding Anna's statement came to light during the interview of Arthur Chatwick. Chatwick was employed by A.J. Cox, who owned the local freight delivery and trash pickup businesses in Stony Brook. Chatwick stated that he had been picking up the trash at the Parsons farm on Mondays, Wednesdays and Fridays for two to three years. When he was questioned regarding his trash pickup at the farm on June 9, he stated that he had arrived to collect the trash at 9:30 a.m. He was quite sure of the time because he had a regular route and arrived at each location at approximately the same time on each pickup day. He confirmed that there was usually a large can of trash in the back of the house near the Pyrex gas tanks. In addition, there were usually a small tub and a small foot-lever can in the kitchen under the sink. He went on to state that he usually went into the kitchen and got these two small trash containers and brought them out to his helper on the truck. In a subsequent interview with Special Agent J.R. O'Hair, Cox indicated that the procedure for trash pickup at the Parsons home for the past four years was to first go into the kitchen and pick up the trash from the foot-lever can and other containers and then go around to the back of the house to collect the big can.

On June 9, 1937, Arthur's helper was a young man by the name of George Minfield, who was a relatively new employee. The normal trash pickup procedure was for Arthur Chatwick to enter the kitchen and retrieve the two small trash cans and bring the cans to George, and George would then empty the items into the trash truck. However, on the morning of June 9, something had changed. On this day when he arrived at the farm, the two small trash containers from the kitchen had already been emptied into the big can before his arrival and were sitting empty outside the house. He stated that this had never occurred in the past. He added that a woman was in the house and came to the door and handed him two boxes of feathers. The description he provided matched Anna Kupryanova. He did not see or hear anyone else in or outside of the house. When questioned about the position of the Dodge, he stated that the car was in the large detached garage located on the right side of the driveway as one pulled into the farm. He noticed that one of the car's doors was partially opened. He described the car as either tan or brown in color and recalled that the car was parked with its nose at the back of the garage. He went on to assert that had the car been parked in the driveway near the house, he would have been required to back up in order to get his truck around the car. He then stated that there was no question in his mind about not backing up that morning.

Arthur Chatwick's interview revealed two important facts regarding the disappearance of Alice Parsons. First, it is unlikely that Alice was present in the house that morning and holding a door open for Anna as Anna had claimed. Chatwick was convinced that there was no one else present when the woman he believed to be Anna Kupryanova handed him two boxes of feathers that morning. Secondly, either Anna or a second person had moved the Dodge.

This brought to light the next major contradiction regarding both William Parsons's and Anna Kupryanova's prior statements. Those statements had to do with Anna's claimed inability to drive an automobile.

During an FBI interview, Anna's longtime friend Eudoxia Gulovtchick of Bayside, New York, indicated that Anna had written in a letter to her that she had to, at times, drive Roy to school. In addition, Percy Smith, proprietor of the Stony Brook Butcher Store, told the FBI that he had seen Anna driving an automobile on three different occasions. Further investigation produced witnesses Mary L. Jane, Leona Newton and Isabella Vreeland, who all stated that they had witnessed Anna Kupryanova operating an automobile in the past.

The final piece of critical evidence that proved Anna Kupryanova to be lying about her driving ability came during a chance meeting with one of the FBI agents assigned to the case. One afternoon during the course of the investigation, Special Agent G.H. Meyers was having lunch in Bayside, when Bunny Parsons, wife of John Parsons, came into the restaurant with an elderly woman and they seated themselves at a nearby table. Agent Meyers pretended that he did not notice their entrance into the restaurant, but eventually, Bunny Parsons approached him and started discussing certain details of the investigation. During the course of the conversation, Bunny Parsons stated that Anna could positively drive an automobile and that she had obtained an operator's license from the State of New York. She went on to say that she specifically recalled the time when she and her husband, John, waited in the car while Anna took her road test. Anna failed her test that day but returned the following week, passed the road test and obtained her license. Bunny Parsons told Agent Meyers that Anna took her road test approximately two years after entering William and Alice's employment.

It was not only Anna's lies that raised Inspector Connelley's suspicions. William Parsons had made several statements early on in the investigation that made Connelley question William's truthfulness. The first lie Parsons told the police occurred within the first five minutes of Lieutenant Stacey Williams's arrival, when William introduced Anna Kupryanova as his sister, Anna Parsons. This was patently false. Although the statement was corrected later, it is unclear why William felt the need to tell such a lie. William also claimed that he had legally adopted Anna's son, Roy, when in reality Anna was opposed to any such adoption because of the potential for the loss of her parental rights. Roy and Anna had simply been granted the right in their citizenship applications to use the name *Parsons*. This was done with the supposed approval of both William and Alice. Another deep concern was William's response when he was asked about Anna's ability to drive an automobile. He stated that she was just beginning to learn. However, as confirmed by Bunny Parsons, Anna had taken and passed her road test almost five years before Alice's disappearance.

During the late evening hours of June 9, Brookhaven police officer John Harding interviewed William Parsons regarding his home relationship with his wife, Alice. In that interview, William claimed that there had been no arguments between them and that he and his wife lived perfectly. However, less than three hours later, during an interview with Investigator Morris, William told Morris that for the past six or eight weeks, his wife had not spoken to him sometimes for half a day at a time. This trouble, he stated, arose over the other woman. He told Morris that he believed Anna to be a brighter woman than his wife and Anna had taken over the home and the garden. Another disturbing contradiction arose in that interview. William claimed that he had only traveled into New York City once that year, but in reality, his personal diary indicated that he had been to New York City four times in the past thirty days.

Another issue regarding William's prior statement troubled Inspector Connelley greatly. This involved the circumstances surrounding William's purchase of the *New York Times* on the morning of June 9 at the St. James train station. William claimed in his statement to Inspector Connelley on June 11 that when he had entered the stationery store to buy a copy of the *Times* he immediately noticed two or three strange men who had the disheveled appearance of individuals who had been up all night. The man behind the counter also had the same appearance. In an interview with Special Agents Boyle and Dennis, William Parsons never mentioned these men in the store when he discussed buying the newspaper to read on the train. Subsequent questioning on this issue showed that William kept vacillating as to the actual number of unsavory characters that were in the stationery store that morning. He first claimed the number to be three and in a subsequent interview lowered the number to two. He then changed his story again and stated that only one disheveled man was in the store that morning. After multiple interviews of possible witnesses at the train station and stationery store, it was determined that William Parsons was alone in the store when he purchased his newspaper.

The question that kept being raised in the mind of Inspector Connelley was why William and Anna kept lying about small things.

Inspector Connelley was constantly on the lookout for any lies of omission. William Parsons had repeated several times that once he arrived at the St. James train station on the evening of June 9, he had gone directly to the taxi stand. However, a witness by the name of Louis Libby of Woodlawn Avenue, St. James, identified a photograph of William Parsons as being the man he saw inside the Smith's Stationery store that evening at approximately 7:35 p.m. Libby stated in an interview with Agent G.H. Meyer that he was inside the Smith's Stationery store, which was located just opposite the St. James train station. He stated that Parsons, on entering the store, inquired, "Use your phone?" and then held up a coin in his fingers. The owner of the store, Mr. Smith, pointed to the phone booth in the rear of the store. Parsons had walked quickly to the booth and remained there for a short time. Libby stated that Parsons appeared nervous and excited. Libby was sure of the time because he had purchased a newspaper and had just checked his watch.

Another foundational part of William's and Anna's narratives about the events of June 9 had to do with the statements of Roy Parsons. Roy's first interview took place in the evening of June 9, when Lieutenant Stacey Wilson interviewed him in his room. Wilson had just finished interviewing Anna and had then moved to the stairs. There is no doubt that Anna Kupryanova was well aware that he was on his way up the stairs to interview her son. During the interview with Lieutenant Wilson, Roy indicated that the last time he saw Alice was at breakfast that morning. At a subsequent interview several days later conducted by Special Agents Ward and Schroeder, Roy indicated that he had seen Alice in her car on his way to school on his bicycle. He claimed he saw her within several hundred feet of the farm as she was returning from the St. James train station. The truthfulness of this statement soon came into question when in a subsequent hidden microphone recording of a conversation between William and Anna, the following shocking fact was revealed:

Anna: "You drove to the station in the morning."
William: "That is what they say. But you know that isn't so."

As the investigation moved forward, it became evident that the more William and Anna spoke, the more lies that they would tell. With this in mind, Inspector Connelley devised the first of several ruses that he hoped would expose their lies and perhaps have them turn on each other. Under the tightest of secrecy, this plan was to involve the surreptitious removal of both William and Anna from Long Meadow Farm in the early morning hours of June 24, 1937.

At 4:15 a.m., Agents Martin, O'Hair, Lord, Malone and Treadwell met on the corner of Gould Road and Jericho Turnpike. While the other FBI agents waited, Martin and O'Hair drove to the vicinity of the Parsons farm, parked in a wooded area and proceeded unobserved on foot to the house. William Parsons was awakened by Agents Boyle and Dennis, who were stationed inside the home, and they then met with the newly arrived agents. Agent Martin explained that because the deadline set by William for receipt of a message from the kidnapper was noon that day, it was expected that reporters, local officials and curiosity seekers would converge on the farm at the time of the deadline. He suggested that William might wish to consider being someplace else when the time of the deadline was reached. Additionally, Martin informed William that a new letter had been received and they needed to bring William to a location where the new message could be safely discussed. In reality, this letter was just one of the many attempted extortion letters that had been sent to the Parsons family since Alice's disappearance. However, its arrival could be used to assist the FBI in its ruse to get William to a place where he could be interrogated with little risk of exposure or interruption.

William agreed to leave with the agents. Agents Martin and O'Hair, accompanied now by Agent Boyle, left the house and again traveled unobserved through the wooded area that led to the agents' car. They drove back to the intersection of Gould Road and Jericho Turnpike. At the intersection, Special Agent Martin left the car he had been riding in and entered the car containing Agents Lord, Malone and Treadwell. This second car now returned to the farm. It was their intention to repeat the clandestine movements to move Anna in the same way they had moved William. By 5:15 a.m., Anna Kupryanova was in a car with Agents Lord and Dennis. They were on their way to join their fellow agents and William Parsons at the New York office of the FBI. What they didn't know was that SAC Whitley and a polygraph examiner were waiting for them at that New York City office.

Special Agents Martin, Malone and Treadwell remained in the house in an effort to show activity within the home should it be placed under surveillance by the press or the local police. To add credence to this charade, and to better mask the short-term disappearance of William and Anna, Inspector Connelley remained in this Stony Brook office for the first half of the day. He and SAC Whitley would later switch locations, allowing Connelley another opportunity to question both William and Anna.

While William and Anna were being driven to New York City, Alice's brother Frank McDonell returned to the Parsons home from visiting friends. Today was the day that Frank had agreed to meet with a delegation from the press. Just after the deadline to the kidnappers had passed, this press delegation made a formal request of Frank McDonell. This group included representatives from the *New York Evening Journal*, the Associated Press and the *Herald Tribune* and a photographer from the *Daily Mirror*. They advised McDonell that they did not wish to congregate and cause confusion and suggested that William Parsons set a specific time at which a delegation from the press might speak with him and receive any news or statement he might care to release. Frank McDonell cordially listened to the request and told them he would consider the matter and discuss it with his brother and Parsons.

The press request was relayed to Inspector Connelley at his Stony Brook office, and the inspector suggested that the following statement be released by Frank McDonell:

> *Mrs. Parsons has not returned. We appreciated everything the press has done to aid us in this. We hope that you will continue to cooperate with us so far as is possible. Mr. Parsons at this time would rather not make any statement. However, if at any later time he thinks this will assist, he will do so, and he wants to assure you he wishes to cooperate with you. We have nothing we can offer in the way of suggestions as to how you may assist us. We know you will assist us in every way possible at any time, and we will keep this in mind for future consideration, and will communicate to you our future wishes.*
>
> *We would prefer that no picture be taken at this time. We also request your consideration in contacting us in the future. I would suggest that you communicate to me any subsequent request through one of your members—anything you may have in mind.*

At two o'clock that afternoon, the same delegation of press representatives again met with Frank McDonell. Frank had copied the statement into his own handwriting before he read it to the press. After the reading of the statement, several requests were made for photographs of Anna Kupryanova. These requests were politely refused. It was then agreed that the press would call two times per day for updates or questions. One call would be made in the morning, and one call would be made in the afternoon.

The interviews at the New York offices were initially handled by SAC Whitley and polygraph examiner F.P. Coffey. In addition to the polygraph examinations, the purpose behind bringing William and Anna to the FBI's New York office had three underlying goals. These were 1) elicit additional lies, 2) elicit admissions as to past lies and 3) plant a seed of doubt in William's mind about Anna's innocence in the disappearance of Alice Parsons.

It was 9:40 p.m. on the night of June 24 when Inspector E.J. Connelley began his interview of Anna Kupryanova. During this interview, Connelley confronted Anna with the fact that notepaper containing the same watermark as the ransom note had been found in Roy's room. He also told her that it had been purchased in a Woolworth's store in the village of Patchogue. Anna eventually admitted to being in that particular store and buying writing paper. She stated in the interview that she and Roy had recently attended the picture show *The Prince and the Pauper* at the Patchogue Theater. While they were in Patchogue, Mr. and Mrs. Parsons had left them to do some shopping, and she and Roy entered the Woolworth's store. She went on to state that she had made a purchase at the stationery counter of some Fifth Avenue linen paper that was packaged in cellophane. She flatly denied that she or Roy had ever purchased a writing tablet similar to the one containing paper on which the ransom note was written.

Anna had been asked numerous times, during exhaustive interviews and in various ways, if she and William were involved in a romantic or sexual relationship. Her answers were always the same, and she was firm in her denials. In this particular interview, Anna attempted to convince Inspector Connelley that she had a boyfriend in Belgrade, Yugoslavia. She claimed that she had been in contact with him by letter for the past nine years and that the young man was constantly asking her to come to Yugoslavia so that they could be married. She stated that he worked as an electrician and that she had gone to school with his sister. Later in the same interview, Anna reiterated her oft-repeated statement that William and Alice Parsons were a happily married couple and had never quarreled.

At 11:30 p.m., Inspector Connelley began his interview with William Parsons. Connelley began by confronting William regarding the fact that the ransom note had been written on paper that had come from his house. He also confronted him with the fact that Anna had lied to him about Roy's father and that Roy was an illegitimate child. This news appeared to have a considerable effect on William. Connelley told William that it was his belief that Anna had been involved in Alice's disappearance and that William should have a direct conversation with Anna about her involvement and get the truth from her. Connelley then told William that he had made arrangements for William to have a private conversation with Anna immediately following the interview. Both William and Anna had been kept unaware of each other's presence at the FBI office, and William was quite surprised when he was quickly ushered into another room where he found Anna waiting for him. Of course, the private conversation between William and Anna would not be so private in light of the fact that the FBI had planted hidden microphones in the room.

It was clear from the onset of William and Anna's conversation that they believed someone was attempting to listen to them. Although completely alone behind a closed door, they still whispered to each other. With the closest microphone three feet away, only portions of their conversation could be heard by the monitoring FBI agents. Such portions of the conversation as could be heard were as follows:

William: "They tell me the paper comes out of the house."
Anna: "I know. If you do not do anything you do not know it."
Anna: "I don't know anything about the paper. I do not deny the paper for one minute came from our house, but I never saw the paper."

In addition to the interviews, both Anna and William were subjected to polygraph examinations conducted by Coffey and witnessed by SAC Whitley. Unfortunately, the results of these examinations were inconclusive. Anna Kupryanova was asked forty-four questions during four separate blocks of questioning. In regards to her examination results, the examiner reported:

> *During the questioning many pronounced emotional reactions were reflected on the polygraphs. In light of this it was not possible to isolate any of these reactions to where they would point strongly that the woman was actually a participant in either a kidnapping or a murder.*

William Parsons's polygraph produced similar results. After fifty-three questions during six blocks of questioning, the examiner's report stated:

> *There was nothing found in studying the emotional reactions of this man to indicate any specific guilty knowledge of participation in this crime. In this respect, however, it should be noted that he is not what is usually considered*

a good subject for the polygraph in that his reactions are not sufficiently pronounced to permit very ready detection.

The polygraph technology of the time was, as it is today, considered unreliable and of limited use in a criminal investigation. The best example of this can be seen in William Parsons's response to two of the questions that were asked of him during the polygraph exam. When asked if the dogs were present on the farm the morning that Alice disappeared, he replied, "Yes." When asked if his feelings for Anna were of a sisterly or platonic nature he also replied, "Yes." By the measurements used in determining the polygraph's results, both of the answers were considered truthful. However, one of these answers would soon be exposed as a bald-faced lie.

Both William and Anna were returned to Long Meadow Farm by the FBI in the early morning hours on June 25. There were no witnesses to their arrival, and it appeared that no one had been aware of their lengthy absence. William made a note in his diary for that day. He wrote, "Anna and I taken to New York FBI headquarters, and questioned all night until 5 a.m., Friday, when we got home."

In an internal memo to Director Hoover, Assistant Director Tamm noted that "the idea of Anna being involved had been planted in Parsons' mind and he questioned her, but she denies implication to him as well."

Inspector Connelley returned to his Stony Brook office that morning and opened a report that was awaiting him. It was FBI Laboratory Report #7-1974-195, and it informed him that, after careful handwriting analysis, the laboratory had determined that Howard McDonell, Frank McDonell, William Parsons and Roy Parsons had not written the original ransom note. This conclusion was based on handwriting specimens for these individuals that had been forwarded to the laboratory on June 21. The laboratory further advised that no conclusion had been reached from a comparison of the known hand printing of Anna Kupryanova with the hand printing in the original note. The report went on to state that some of her specimens showed similarities to the text in the ransom note, but additional handwriting specimens from Anna Kupryanova would be needed.

Family members continued to come and go at the Parsons home. Just before Frank McDonell and his wife, Emily, were to return to New Jersey, they met privately in a room with Agents Malone and Martin. Emily wanted to tell the agents that in October 1922 she had been in London, England, where she first met William Parsons. She had met William through a Mr. and Mrs. Hay. Mr. Hay was a former classmate of William's at Yale. Emily suggested that the agents find Mr. Hay and speak with him. Mr. Hay had relayed to Emily that William had great difficulty with women and that he had been asked to move by several different landlords.

Just after Frank and Emily McDonell left the Parsons home, Molly Parsons arrived for an extended stay. Molly was soon joined by Alice's aunt Bess Williams. Aunt Bess had practically raised Alice and claimed she would not rest until Alice was found. Also, after the death of her brother Colonel Williams, she held the mortgage to the farm. One of the first things that Aunt Bess did upon her arrival was take inventory of Alice's personal possessions. When going through Alice's clothing, she noticed that one of Alice's handmade nightgowns was missing. Aunt Bess knew this particular piece of clothing well: she had made it for Alice as a gift. She told the FBI agents inside the home that Alice was not in the practice of disposing of such articles and thought that it possible she might have been wearing this article of clothing had she been disposed of during the night of June 8. Aunt Bess made it clear that she did not believe a word of William's and Anna's stories. Adding to her suspicions was the fact that William had told her that Anna wanted the FBI out of the house as quickly as possible.

The end of June also saw a visit from William's brother John and his wife, Bunny. During their visit, they had several conversations with Anna Kupryanova. In a later interview with Special Agent Meyer, Bunny Parsons spoke about one of her conversations with Anna. During that conversation, Anna had claimed that Alice had suffered a miscarriage three or four years ago and had been attended by a doctor at Port Jefferson Hospital. Anna also claimed that Alice suffered terrific pains at times during her menstrual cycles.

Bunny went on to say that she was aware of the fact that Alice had always evidenced a desire for children and seemed very happy and elated at the time that she (Bunny) and her husband, John, adopted a son in May 1935. She said that both William and Alice seemed to have an attitude of sadness about the adoption and, upon seeing the adopted baby for the first time, began to cry. Bunny noted that Alice was generally not an emotional person and appeared to be dispassionate, evidencing no desire for sexual indulgence.

JULY 1937

The month of July opened a new chapter in the investigation of Alice Parsons's disappearance. New evidence developed, and old lies were exposed. The first major development came as a complete surprise to the FBI. It appeared that local law enforcement had been busier that the bureau had believed.

On July 7, Assistant District Attorney Lindsay Henry called on Inspector Connelley at the FBI's Stony Brook office. Henry advised Connelley that the District Attorney's Office had consulted with the handwriting experts Osborne and Osborne of 233 Broadway, New York City. The principal of this firm, Albert Sherman Osborne, was the leading expert in the country when it came to questionable document examinations. He had offered his scientific opinion in numerous criminal cases, including the Lindbergh kidnapping just a few years before. In an announcement that shocked Inspector Connelley, Henry informed him that Osborne and his son had examined a photostatic copy of the ransom note and examples of Anna Kupryanova's handwriting and was of the opinion that Kupryanova had written the note.

This caused an immediate stir at the FBI headquarters in Washington, D.C. In a memo from Director Hoover to his assistant Tamm at ten o'clock that evening, Hoover wrote:

> *Mr. Connelley telephoned from Stony Brook, Long Island, and stated that he had determined from Henry that they had secured an off-hand opinion from both Osborne and his son that the note is in the handwriting of the woman. Mr. Connelley stated they were riding along until they get a formal opinion on the real note; that Hill and Henry are to meet him, Connelley, at noon tomorrow. Mr. Connelley stated he had explained to Henry today the inadvisability of taking some half-cocked action and eliminating the possibility of anything in the future. I stated that if the Osborne decision is that the woman wrote the note and they go ahead and arrest her and she should confess, it would take the thing right from under us.*

The following morning at 9:45 a.m., Director Hoover again sent a memorandum to Tamm regarding the Osborne situation. In it, he wrote,

> *Mr. Connelley stated that the local authorities have taken photostatic copies of the note and have taken it to Osborne and have obtained from him apparently a fairly definite opinion that it is in Anna's handwriting. Mr. Connelley stated that Henry had said nothing about a definite identification, apparently waiting until Osborne could see the original which they have requested and which he is to show him today. I stated he, Connelley, should*

take the note over so that they cannot put us in the position of holding out on them. I stated that if Osborne makes the identification of the Russian and under questioning she may break….Mr. Connelley stated that he believed the Osbornes would make a definite decision that the note was in the Russian woman's handwriting and that as a matter of fact, he, Connelley, had no doubt personally that the note was written by her….Mr. Connelley stated that they had made up a Russian transcript of the note and had asked the woman to translate it into English; that today she produced an entirely new system of printing, in a sort of script type. Mr. Connelley stated she knew what they were after and he has no doubt that she is trying to deceive them as to her printing.

Later that morning, Inspector Connelley spoke with both District Attorney Hill and Assistant District Attorney Henry regarding the potential arrest of Anna Kupryanova in response to the Osbornes' findings. During the conversation Connelly reminded Hill and Henry that they had already confronted Anna about her having written the ransom note. The only thing that had changed was that an outside party might now concur with their opinion. Connelley felt that concurrence might not be enough to convince Anna Kupryanova that she should surrender herself and tell the authorities where Alice's body was located. By the end of the telephone conversation with Connelley, both Hill and Henry agreed to keep the investigation on its present course, regardless of whether or not the Osbornes made a definite identification of the ransom note's author.

Another unique situation arose in the beginning of July. Special Agent L.G. Turrou had been brought into the case from the Washington, D.C field office. Inspector Connelley specifically requested Turrou because of his ability to speak the Russian language fluently. Agent Turrou arrived at the Parsons home on July 3 accompanied by Inspector Connelley. After the usual introductions, Agent Turrou began to interview Anna Kupryanova in her native language. Anna continued to tell her usual lies regarding her marriages, the death of Hans Soni in a car accident and the parentage of her son. However, in this interview, Anna added a new element that was a major change from her previous recitations: Anna now claimed, after a dozen previous interviews, that when Alice arrived home from dropping William off at the train station, she appeared to be extremely nervous and was not acting normal. Anna noted, as an example, that when Alice wiped the dishes in the kitchen, she had placed them in the incorrect position in the closet. Anna said it was apparent that Alice's mind was on something else.

Anna also claimed, in complete contradiction to her previous statements, that William and Alice had frequent arguments that would last until the early morning hours, and these arguments were in connection with the fact that Alice wanted a child of her own. Anna claimed to have been in their presence when William told Alice that he was fifty years of age and that it was late for her to bear any children. He stated that he believed he would not live to see his children grow up. Anna went on to say that Alice's desire to have children was so profound that she had shown signs of mental derangement. Anna cited as an example the times when Alice, anticipating pregnancy, would start knitting socks and sweaters for her expected infant, but with the reappearance of her menstrual periods, she would immediately fall into a state of despondency and melancholy. She would then gather up the infant clothing she had knitted and sell the items at a nearby exchange.

Anna, who had always professed to believe that Alice had been kidnapped, now suggested that Alice may have arranged with some unknown person to take her away from the farm to make it appear that she had been kidnapped. Anna stated that she now believed that Alice had prepared the ransom note found in her car in advance, believing that William would pay the $25,000 immediately. She claimed that Alice would then use the money for living expenses and would eventually return to divorce her husband, with whom she apparently no longer wished to live.

Anna also now questioned the mental stability of William Parsons. She claimed that William had told her that if it had not been for young Roy, to whom he was much attached, he would have long ago committed suicide. He also said that he felt at fault for Alice's' disappearance, due to the fact that he could not satisfy Alice with relation to her great desire to bear a child. This telling interview with the iron-willed Anna Kupryanova ended with her usual emphatic denial that she had ever been intimate with William Parsons.

On July 8, William went to visit his sister Laura Pratt in Glen Cove for a luncheon and a swim. This provided another opportunity for Agent Turrou and Anna Kupryanova to have a lengthy conversation in her native language. During the course of this conversation, it was clear that Anna was again attempting to alter the narrative she had provided in a dozen previous interviews. She began by adding an element of violence to her recent claim that the Parsonses quarreled every day of the week, saying that at times the quarrels became so violent that they bordered on fistfights. Anna claimed that at one point, Alice shouted that she did not want to go on living and would prefer to be dead. Anna then suggested that Mrs. Parsons may have run off with some young man, and she didn't think she would be returning.

It also became clear during the conversation that Anna had resigned herself to the fact that the ransom paper was found in the house, but she insisted that Alice must have written the note. Anna stated that the reason for the similarity between the handwriting on the note and hers was because Alice had taught her to print. In a surprising and baffling reversal of one of Anna's key month-long denials, she admitted to Special Agent Turrou that she could drive an automobile.

This admission on Anna Kupryanova's part was critical to Inspector Connelley's investigation. Connelley knew that there was a blank period of time on the morning Alice disappeared. It had always been the normal routine in the Parsons home for Alice to answer the telephone and greet all visitors. Yet on the day she disappeared, Alice did not appear from 8:00 a.m. onward. The investigation determined that Mr. Elderkin, the St. James butcher, had called at 9:30 a.m. and Anna had answered the telephone. A short time after that, trash collector Arthur Chatwick arrived at the house and found the empty kitchen cans sitting outside and Anna Kupryanova standing at the door. Then at approximately 11:32 a.m., Mr. Ketchum, the stationmaster at the Stony Brook train station, called regarding Mr. Parsons's farm wagon. When he called, Anna answered the telephone.

It was now Inspector Connelley's theory that the car had been moved on the morning of June 9 and had been driven by Anna to transport Alice's body to some unknown location. There were still many unanswered questions in Connelley's mind; however, the key questions were how Alice was overcome, and the motivation behind such a violent action. Those answers were soon to come.

Inspector Connelley began to press hard. He sensed a weakening in William Parsons's resolve, compounded by the continuous altering of the narrative as told by Anna Kupryanova. He was now aware that each time he spoke with William and Anna, something new could, and probably would, be learned. His plan now was to begin another lengthy round of questioning. This time, the subject would be the matter of the missing chloroform. This was the half-filled bottle of chloroform that Lieutenant Stacey Wilson had seen in the kitchen on the night of Alice's disappearance. Although the bottle had gone missing that evening, Wilson was able to recall the label information. He had later gone to Kane's Drug Store in Port Jefferson and checked the poison sales records. He had also interviewed the druggist Harry Kane. He found out that William Parsons had entered Kane's Drug Store fifteen days before Alice's disappearance and purchased a two-ounce bottle of chloroform from him.

On July 9, at 7:40 p.m., Inspector Connelley, Agent Turrou, William Parsons and stenographer Nathaniel Bodinger sat in an upstairs room of the Parsons' farmhouse. Inspector Connelley turned to Agent Turrou and said, "Bring him upstairs."

Agent Turrou left the room and retuned a minute later with Harry Kane, the druggist and owner of Kane's Drug Store in Port Jefferson. Inspector Connelley asked Kane if the man sitting in the room was the same man who claimed to be William Parsons in his store and who had purchased a bottle of chloroform. Kane said that he was the same man. That answer prompted William Parsons to state, "I have never seen you before in my life, Mr. Kane."

After a brief discussion between Inspector Connelley and Kane, William Parsons again denied ever meeting the druggist. William stated emphatically, "You know and I know that you have never seen me before in your life, and I have never seen you before."

Kane was then asked to leave the room. Inspector Connelley then said to William, "Well, we are now at the crossroads of something very serious. I don't know what it is, and you are the only one that can help us. The whole thing is in your hand now."

William replied, "I beg your pardon, Mr. Connelley, I never saw that man before and I never bought that chloroform."

Connelley responded, "That is so very inconsistent—with the same situation we get down on the newsstand. You see two men, you see three men…" Connelley then tried to clarify William Parsons's situation by saying, "You take the man and turn his records out, and there is the sale of it to Mr. Parsons, plus the records of the filling of the prescriptions, which there was no question came here also. You see it's a lot of damnable circumstances even though you were not there."

William responded, "But I wasn't there. That shows the man is lying."

Connelley then said, "The man isn't lying, because this man in his first interview, showed his records, and he showed there Mr. Parsons, right on the book, Stony Brook, received two ounces of chloroform on May 24, 12:15 p.m. right at noon, and it was an incidental purchase. It wasn't something that you went in there for. It was an incidental purchase, because of the fact that an order had been left to fill the prescription and you called for the prescription. Incidental to the prescription being handed to you, you then presumable of course that you are the man that was there, said, 'Give me two ounces of chloroform,' and you gave what he believed was a plausible reason for doing it, and he took for granted that you were Mr. Parsons of

Stony Brook because you said you were....We were in doubt as to how he would know whether it was you or not till he looked at you, and there is no question between the two of you, you and Turrou, that you were the man."

William, maintaining his denial, replied, "I tell you I wasn't the man. I didn't buy it."

Agent Turrou then joined the conversation and said, "I just talked to your doctor, and he expressed his opinion officially that two ounces of chloroform will stupefy and render unconscious any person, and it all depends upon the person whether it would cause death."

After a short break, William Parsons continued to insist that he had not purchased the chloroform. He went on, "It must have been a case of mistaken identity. I know I wasn't the man. I know he didn't sell it to me."

Connelley then asked, "Well, if it's a case of mistaken identity, who do you think the man would be that would come in under the name of William H. Parsons and get the medicine belonging to Anna at the same time and subsequently this bottle is found at the estate—who would be the man to have bought this and have brought it down here?"

William again replied, "I don't know, it wasn't me."

Inspector Connelley had one more card to play that evening. As intended, he ended his interview with William Parsons with this final piece of information. He said, "Another thing, Anna told us the story that her husband was that Hindi, Soni, was found dead or had met with an accident in the south of France. We checked up on it yesterday and today and received definite information that he is very well and alive."

While William Parsons rested, Inspector Connelley turned his attention to Anna Kupryanova, who was waiting for him in a downstairs room. With Agent Turrou and the stenographer present, Connelley began his questioning regarding the purchase of the chloroform. As he had with William Parsons just a few minutes before, Connelley went step by step through the facts, which included Anna standing next to the bottle of chloroform in the kitchen and her prescriptions being picked up at Kane's Drug Store at the same time the chloroform was purchased.

Anna Kupryanova, just as William Parsons had done earlier, disavowed any knowledge of the purchase of chloroform or ever even having a seen a bottle of chloroform in the house. Inspector Connelley told both William and Anna that had they simply offered a plausible explanation for the purchase of the chloroform, the matter would probably have been dropped. It was their denials that fed the investigation. As he told them both, "When people begin to deny things, then the thing becomes important."

During the interviews on July 9, both William and Anna were allowed to speak privately with each other, with a promise from William that he would try to get something out of Anna and a promise from Anna that she would try to have William admit something. They were then placed in a private room that was being electronically monitored. Once they were together, they immediately began to counsel each other against making any admissions. Inspector Connelley now believed, based on the chloroform incident, that William Parsons and Anna Kupryanova were guilty in the murder of Alice Parsons.

On July 11 at 6:00 a.m., William and Anna were bundled into a bureau car and transported to the FBI office in New York City. Inspector Connelley believed that the pressure was finally reaching William Parsons and that William was on the verge of making a confession. Inspector Connelley was so confident of the day's outcome that he invited J. Edgar Hoover to the New York office.

While William and Anna were being questioned at the FBI's New York office, a news report came in regarding the discovery of a body of a woman wearing a blue dress floating in Long Island Sound. Inspector Connelley strongly suggested to William that it was the body of Alice Parsons and that undoubtedly an autopsy would show that she probably was killed and chloroform had been administered in connection with her death.

This news had an immediate effect on William Parsons. He became quiet and withdrawn and remained that way for some time. Finally, William appeared to have come to a decision and asked to speak with Inspector Connelley immediately.

William was brought to a room where he met privately with Connelley. Parsons began, "I have nothing to live for. Can I say to you that I killed my wife, that I chloroformed her?" Parsons then said, "I want to protect Roy. He is not able to understand what is going on." Parsons then insisted again that he wanted to say that he killed his wife and that he would plead guilty. He wanted to know what would happen to him and if he could be executed right away to finally get this thing over with.

Connelley told him he could not plead guilty to first-degree murder without the facts being heard. He was also told that due to the incident with the chloroform and the ransom note left by Anna that they both would have to be placed on trial. Parsons then insisted that he was responsible for Alice's death, but he did not kill her.

At 7:35 p.m. that evening, William Parsons made, after a full month of repeated and unwavering denials, an important revelation to Inspector

Connelley. It was a revelation that could easily provide a motive for the disappearance of Alice Parsons. William said, "You know Anna and I have been living together as man and wife. This has been going on for years. We used contraceptives which had been purchased by me."

Connelley already knew this. Alice's desire for a child and her limiting of sexual contact to procreation purposes ruled out the possibility of contraceptive use for her and William. However, special agents had found one of the farmhouse's cesspools loaded with used condoms. Parsons then stated to Connelley, "I could see that this growing affection of Anna for me and her resentment of Mrs. Parsons could lead to no other end than disaster in connection with the relationship of the three grown persons in one house."

Parsons went on to explain that the situation inside the home became so strained as a result of his close relationship with Anna that it came to pass that he had been unable to indicate any affection toward Alice without Anna quarreling with him. She was constantly resentful, and if he wished to show any affection toward his wife, he would have to do it outside Anna's presence. He then stated, "I believe, therefore, I am responsible for my wife's death by reason of allowing this to go on. I could see that my wife was not inclined toward these things. In fact it was repulsive to her, and I am oversexed. Anna is oversexed." William then claimed that Alice had been opposed to any intimate relationship between a man and wife unless its purpose was to create a child and that this cold attitude had pushed him into an intimate relationship with Anna.

William Parsons continued to be questioned that evening. At one point, the questioning was taken over by Special Agent Turrou. With Agent Turrou, Inspector Connelley and a third witness in the interview room, Parsons admitted that he had purchased the chloroform in Port Jefferson on May 24 and that Anna had gone with him on this day to get her prescription filled. He stated that she remained seated in the car while he went in to pick up the prescription and purchase the chloroform. Parsons made this admission to Special Agent Turrou, who was sitting across the table from him alongside Inspector Connelley. The third witness in the room was Director J. Edgar Hoover of the FBI.

Later during the interview, William spoke about Alice's trip to California the previous October to attend her brother's wedding. Anna had objected to William writing letters to Alice, which resulted in a heated argument between him and Anna. The argument resulted in Anna threatening to leave him. He then stated that he had succeeded in persuading her to remain at the farm and that he had reassured her that when Alice returned he would straighten it all out. He then said to Anna, "Two is company and three is a crowd."

Parsons then spoke about a special contract that had been drawn up between Anna, Alice and himself the previous fall. He stated that the reason for the contract was that Anna had indicated that she was going to England and that in order to keep her from leaving he agreed to the contract. It was a contract whereby Anna was to receive $25,000 from their estate in case of the death of one of them and the marriage of the survivor. Parsons claimed that Anna dominated him in the preparation of the contract and had chosen the amount herself. He then said that he, in turn, had pressured Alice into signing the contract, as he had dominated her in all matters. The contract was prepared by William and Alice's local attorney, Theron Sammis of Huntington. Sammis had advised William that he was tying himself into a knot by signing this contract and strongly recommended against signing. Sometime later, William had a change of heart and tore up all copies of the contract. It did not go unnoticed by Inspector Connelley that the $25,000 guaranteed to Anna Kupryanova in the now-broken contract was the same amount demanded in the ransom note on June 9 (the ransom note written on paper found within the farmhouse and reportedly written in the hand of Anna Kupryanova).

Throughout William Parsons's lengthy interview that evening, he continually vacillated over details of his admissions. At times, he claimed that he went into Kane's Drug Store to pick up the chloroform. At other times, he said that Anna had gone into the store alone. In order to secure a final account from him, Inspector Connelley requested that Parsons provide a sworn statement. The statement was in the format of questions and answers recorded by an FBI stenographer.

The key questions asked by Inspector Connelley, and Parsons's answers, were as follows:

NEW YORK CITY
JULY 12, 1937

STATEMENT OF WILLIAM H. PARSONS, STONY BROOK, NEW YORK, MADE TO INSPECTOR E.J. CONNELLEY, FEDERAL BUREAU OF INVESTIGATIONS, UNITED STATES DEPARTMENT OF JUSTICE, IN THE PRESENCE OF SPECIAL AGENT LEON TURROU, MADE FREELY AND VOLUNTARILY BY MR. PARSONS.
(As to the chloroform purchase)

Connelley: "Do you say that you were the person who made this purchase, notwithstanding your previous denial to Mr. Kane that you had never seen him before?"

William: "Yes."

Connelley: "Was not your real idea of protection concerned primarily with your belief that Anna was the person who killed Mrs. Parsons?"

William: "Yes."

Connelley: "Knowing that this chloroform had been purchased on May 24, 1937, would this suggest to your mind that Anna might have used this in killing Mrs. Parsons after you had come to believe that Mrs. Parsons had been killed?"

William: "Yes."

Connelley: "Your statement as to having purchased the two ounces of chloroform on May 24 are the same statements in effect as previously made to Mr. Hoover in the presence of myself and Agent Turrou?"

William: "Yes."

Connelley: "Mr. Hoover used no duress or force in making you make any such statement?"

William: "No."

Connelley: "This statement is made voluntarily by you in order to correct any false impressions which you might have made as to this situation previously?"

William: "Yes."

Connelley: "Do you believe, based upon all the developments in this matter since June 9, 1937, that Anna is the person responsible for the death of Mrs. Parsons?"

William: "Yes."

William went on to tell Inspector Connelley that Anna had mentioned several times recently that when the issue of Alice's disappearance was resolved and the money from her estate obtained, she and William could leave the United States and move to Europe or Canada. She also wanted to place Roy in a school in Vancouver. William said he agreed with her plans and had hoped to accompany her. This was in spite of the fact that he now believed that he might be Anna's next victim should he accompany her out of the country. He also claimed that Anna kept repeating that Alice's disappearance was "fate."

It was 3:00 a.m. at the New York office of the FBI, and William was still talking. William now appeared to be in full cooperation mode and seemed to accept the belief that Anna was responsible for killing his wife. William suggested to Inspector Connelley a logical place where Alice might be buried in the woods on the farm. He prepared a diagram of the house, driveway, garden and wooded section and designated a place about ten feet west of the trash dump at the edge of the woods. He designated another place to dig approximately ten yards east of the stone pile. Agents were immediately dispatched to these locations and began to dig. At sunrise that morning, they reported negative results.

Anna Kupryanova had been present at the FBI's New York office all during the period that William was being questioned by Inspector Connelley. By design, she was kept informed as to what William was telling the inspector. She was even shown a copy of William's sworn statement. Once Anna had been made fully aware of William's statements that evening, he and Anna were taken into a large conference room where they confronted each other in the presence of Inspector Connelley.

Anna began the conversation, which went as follows:

Anna: "Bill, why did you say I told you to buy the chloroform? I did not."

William: "Yes, you did, Anna. You asked me to do this in the car on the way over there."

Anna: "I did not. You are trying to do this because ever since you were identified by this man you are scared and you are trying to drag me into it. I never told you to buy the chloroform. Why do you want to drag me into this mess?"

William: "Why don't you tell them where the bottle is?"

Anna: "You should ask me that question. Why do you make this mess?"

William: "We should get together and tell them where the body is."

Anna: "I don't know where the body is. Ever since he was identified as to the chloroform he has been worried with being charged and now he wants to drag me in. Why do you do this?"

(At this point William and Anna were advised that the FBI believed that Alice was probably chloroformed and buried alive.)

William: "Yes, Anna, we should consider Roy."

After the interviews and discussions had taken place, it was apparent that both William and Anna needed sleep. William was taken to the fifth floor, and Anna was taken to the thirtieth floor. Before leaving, Anna addressed Agent Turrou in Russian and told him that she wished to speak with William and that if she was allowed to speak with him for just ten minutes, she would get something out of him that would be of value to the FBI. Of course, the FBI was aware of her use of this shrewd tactic in the past, and the agents were sure her only motive in speaking with William was to dominate him with her will. However, the act of dominance itself had the potential for producing incriminating statements, so they agreed to allow the two to meet.

After being allowed to sleep for about three hours, William and Anna were again taken into a room together. SAC Whitley sat approximately fifty yards away from them and was in a position to watch their physical movements but not hear their conversations. Based on their conversation, it was clear that both William and Anna were unaware of the fact that they were being electronically monitored. This conversation demonstrated the depth of Anna Kupryanova's ironclad will. The conversation could be clearly heard due to the fact that a microphone had been secreted under the very desk at which they were sitting.

William Parsons started the conversation:

William: "I am willing to take the extreme penalty and go to jail."

Anna: "No, Bill. You are not. Do what I tell you, you understand? That's all there is to it. You can't go to jail, Bill. I know something you don't know."

William: "That chloroform."

Anna: "There was no chloroform. This is no chloroform of any kind."

William: "They had the bottle that contained chloroform."

Anna: "Did you see it."

William: "Yes…Well, I didn't see it, but they got it."

Anna: "They don't have it. I destroyed the bottle. That's me to blame… neither you nor I. Why did you tell them all those things?"

William: "I am guilty, not you."

Anna: "No."

William: "Why take the rap. I take the blame. It is obvious I did it because I did do it. I did it.

Anna: "Bill, you didn't do that because there is no body."

Parsons: "Don't say that. Alice didn't go in the air. Tell me what happened."

Anna: "I didn't murder her. I did not. You know it.

William: "I think you must be making a mistake not to tell me whatever you can. I think you do know something you are not telling. I want you to tell me."

Anna: "Yes, I can help you, Bill. What do you want?"

William: "I want the body. What have you done with the body[?]"

Anna: "There is no body."

*****

William: "Why don't you tell me where is Alice?"

Anna: "She is not murdered."

William: "Where is she?"

Anna: "I will tell the lawyer."

William: "Why not tell me?"

Anna: "She is alive. Leave it to me. You are not going to any jail."

William: "Do you know where she is?"

Anna: "Just keep quiet, keep your sense; you must understand what I am telling you."

William: "It's senseless. See the way the world is suspicioning you on the ransom note and the paper in the house."

Anna: "Only yesterday they took it. There is nothing proved. And you, and you lost faith in me in those few hours that you were here."

William: "Where is Alice? Tell me where Alice is. That is all you have to do is tell me what happened."

Anna: "If you are going to shout like this we can't talk this way. There is nothing to it. She went with those people."

William: "Who were they?"

Anna: "I don't know who those people were. The lawyer is going to fix that."

*****

Anna: "Why do you accuse me?"

William: "Who had anything to do with it but you?"

Anna: "I?"

William: "Yes."

Anna: "You drove to the station in the morning."

William: "That is what they say. But you know that isn't so."

Anna: "And you know it isn't so with Alice."

William: "Do you know where she is?"

Anna: "I couldn't tell you those things because you would be blabbing out everything."

*****

William: "Why can't you tell me where Alice is?"

Anna: "Whatever happened to Alice, we are not murderers until murder is proved."

*****

William: "There isn't anything….Mr. Hoover himself is….I don't know why you want a lawyer to find out where Alice is; where the body is."

Anna: "Don't you worry. There is no body."

William: "She isn't around the place anymore."

Anna: "What, have you gone crazy? These people did not mess around—What are you talking about? The people went from one place to another, but they didn't dig all the ground."

After listening to the conversation between William and Anna, Inspector Connelley was even more convinced of Anna's control and dominance over

William Parsons. Connelley also believed that William was sincere in his efforts to find out what happened to Alice. Yet at the same time, he knew that William was holding back a great deal of information in an effort to protect Anna. The reason for this protection, as William would soon admit to his brother John, was that he was in love with Anna Kupryanova.

William Parsons and Anna Kupryanova finally left the FBI's New York office during the late afternoon on July 13, 1937. They left in separate cars, with William being driven by Inspector Connelley to his brother's house in Bayside and Anna being driven to their home in Stony Brook. When William arrived at this brother John's home, John introduced William to Ben Shiverts, Anna Kupryanova's new attorney.

Connelley later noted that both William and Anna were entirely friendly after the vigorous questioning that they had been subjected to while in the New York City office. However, he was also cognizant of the fact that Anna may have been considerably pleased and satisfied with her own efforts in thwarting the bureau's efforts to obtain hard evidence against them. It was now clear that the iron-willed Anna Kupryanova believed that if there was no chloroform bottle, then there could be no chloroform, and if there was no body, there could be no murder.

When Inspector Connelley and Anna arrived at Long Meadow Farm, they were met by eight cars full of reporters, Assistant District Attorney Henry and District Attorney L. Baron Hill. It was later determined to be nothing more than a publicity event for Hill. Hill wanted to issue a press statement regarding the Parsons case even though there was really no new information that could be released to the public. Without consulting the bureau, and in his effort to obtain publicity, he committed a major blunder that would prove to strengthen the resolve of Anna Kupryanova and weaken all that Connelley had tried to accomplish over the last three days. District Attorney Hill told the gathered reporters that the case could not be solved "until the body of Alice Parsons was found." As Anna had said to William just hours before, "Don't you worry. There is no body."

Two days later, Anna Kupryanova's complete domination over William Parsons showed itself again to Inspector Connelley. Parsons had reached out to Connelley and requested that he immediately come to his Stony Brook home. William said that he wished to make another statement. When Connelley arrived at Long Meadow Farm, William rushed out to meet him. William started talking immediately and said that he was very sorry but he would have to retract his prior sworn statement regarding the chloroform. He said he fully recognized that this would be destroying the possibility of anybody believing his truthfulness in the future. Connelley sat down at William's office typewriter and began to type as William dictated his new statement. In this new statement, he claimed that neither he nor Anna purchased any chloroform from Kane's Drug Store on May 24, 1937. He also retracted all of his statements regarding his personal relationship with Anna Kupryanova. The new statement ended with William claiming, "My reason for saying that I had purchased this chloroform previously when I had not actually purchased the same was in my opinion due entirely to weakness and unmanliness in an effort to save my own skin."

When the statement was complete, Anna was called into the room so that he could show her what had been written. William was very anxious that Anna know that he had fully recanted his previous statement. Anna sat down and began to read William's new statement and, after some criticism as to his having mentioned the May 24 date, she stated she felt the statement was all right. Anna then told Inspector Connelley that she and William were going to leave Long Meadow Farm in order to save Roy from the unpleasant situation. She then began a litany of attacks on the local police and the FBI for the way they conducted themselves during the investigation. It was just the beginning of many such confrontations.

Although Anna Kupryanova believed that forcing William to change his sworn statement was a victory over the FBI, it could only be described as a hollow victory. Both William's and Anna's understanding of the criminal justice system was clearly limited. The "But I took back my incriminating statements" defense has rarely worked in criminal cases such as these. Their long list of lies; the chloroform purchase records; the destruction of the chloroform evidence; the used condoms in the cesspool; and their own words recorded by the hidden microphone at the FBI's New York office could not be wiped away by simply signing a new statement.

Inspector E.J. Connelley was well aware of all of this. However, he was also aware that the evidence they had gathered to date was circumstantial and he needed more. He needed the body of Alice Parsons.

10
Letters from the Kidnappers

One of the most intriguing aspects of the Alice Parsons kidnapping case was the multiple letters that were received from the suspected kidnappers during the summer of 1937. The first letter arrived on July 8, almost a full month after the kidnapping. It was a Special Delivery letter addressed to Mr. William H. Parsons, Stony Brook, Long Island. It had been postmarked the day before at the Hudson Terminal in New York City. The poorly written letter was typed in all capital letters and read as follows:

MR. PARSONS

YOU WILL BE BETTER OFF IF YOU GET RID OF ALL THE COPS YOU HAVE AS YOU WILL GET NO WHERE WITH THEM. YOUR WIFE HAS BEEN AT DEATH DOORS FOR THE LAST. TWENTY FOUR DAYS. BUT TODAY WITH GOOD CARE SHE IS GETTING ALONG FINE. HERE IS THE WAY THINGS HAPPENED. YOUR WIFE WAS KEPT IN A BARN NOT. FAR FROM YOU HOUSE FOR A WEEK OR SO CRYING AND NOT EATING. THERE WAS. NO BATH ROOM OR ANY PRIVACY OF THE WOMAN. THINGS GOT A LITTLE HOT AND WE MADE CONNECTION TO BRING HER TO NEW YORK. AT A BIG EXPENSE WE GOT HERE. THE WOMAN HAD

A BOTH ROOM BUT IT WAS NO GOOD TO HER. SHE COLLAPSED AS SHE ENTERED THE PLACE. WE MADE CONNECTIONS FOR A DOCTOR WHO KNEW WHAT IT WAS ALL ABOUT. HE GOT ANOTHER DOCTOR FRIEND OF HIS AND THE SAID YOU WIFE WAS IN A CRITICAL CONDITION WITH A BAD CASE OF PNEUMONIA. THEY GOT TWO NURSES AND WENT TO WORK. THE NURSES WENT AND BOUGHT NEW CLOTHING FROM HEAD TO FOOT AS HER CLOTHING WAS VERY DIRTY FROM NO PRIVACY. THE NURSES WORKED ONE DAY AND ONE NIGHT AS DID THE DOCTORS. THE WOMAN BECAME SO BAD THAT OXYGEN TANKS WERE ORDERED. SO THE CRISIS CAME AND SHE PASSED IT ALL RIGHT AND TODAY THE NURSE GAVE HER A LITTLE WHITE MEAT AND A SIP OF MILK. ALL THE TIME SHE HAVE BEEN GETTING LIQUID FOOD. SHE WILL TELL YOU BETTER WHEN SHE GET HOME. NOW PLEASE DON'T TRY AND GET FUNNY AS YOU WILL BE THE ONE THAT WILL LOSE. IT WILL TAKE TOO LONG TO TELL YOU ANY MORE SO LET US GET DOWN TO FACTS. FROM THE RESULTS OF WHAT YOU WIFE WENT THROUGH IT LEFT HER WITH A LITTLE BAD HEART GET YOURSELF TOGEATHER AND YOU CAN SETTLE THIS THING I HOPE IN A FEW DAYS. YOU WILL HAVE TO PAY ALL THE EXPENSES OF YOUR WIFE THAT IS ALL WE WANT. WE HAVE ENOUGH HEADACH SINCE WE STARTED AND WE WANT TO GET THE WOMAN BACK TO YOU AS SOON AS POSSIBLE. WE WILL DO BUSINESS WITH YOU ONLY SO DON'T BRING ANYBODY ELSE TO DELAY THINGS MORE. YOUR WIFE IS ONLY 20 MINUTES RIDE FROM THE MUNICIPAL. BUILDING IN NEW YORK. THE COST OF ALL EXPENSES FOR YOU WIFE WILL BE $40,000. WE DON'T WANT A CENT OUT OF IT AS WE ARE GUARD OURSELVES. WHEN WE GIVE THE MONEY WE WILL TAKE YOUR WIFE TO YOU IN A TAXICAB.

ALL YOU DO IS GET THE $20,000 IN $5 BILLS AND $20,000 IN $1 BILLS. YOU WILL PUT THE MONEY UNDER THE BACK SEAT OF YOUR CAR AND BRING

YOUR CAR TO A CERTAIN GARAGE IN N.Y. AND TELL THE GARAGE MAN YOU WANT TO LEAVE THE CAR FOR MR. JONES. WHO WILL CALL FOR IT. IF EVERYTHING IS ALL RIGHT AND THE MONEY IS NOT IN SEREAL NUMBER YOU WELL GET YOUR WIFE IN HALF AN HOUR AFTER YOU LEAVE THE MONEY. AFTER YOU LEAVE YOUR AT THE GARAGE TAKE A LITTLE WALK AWAY FROM THE GARAGE AND WHEN YOU COME BACK YOUR WIFE WILL BE IN FRONT OF THE GARAGE IN A TAXI CAB. PLEASE BRING A HEAVY COAT AS YOU WIFE WILL NEED IT AS SHE HAS ONLY A DRESS ON. BE CAREFUL AND DON'T HANG AROUND THE GARAGE AFTER YOU LEAVE YOUR CAR AS WE STILL BE WATCHING YOU CLOSELY. ANY FALSE MOVES YOU WILL GET YOUR MONEY BACK AND THE THING IS ALL OVER. HERE IS YOUR INSTRUCTIONS TO SAVE DELAY YOU GO TO THE DAILY NEWSPAPER AN INSERT HIS IN EVERY MORNING TILL I SEND YOU A LETTER TELLING YOU THE DAY AND TIME TO LEAVE YOUR CAR AT THE GARAGE. I WILL GIVE YOU THE ADDRESS.

HERE IS WHAT YOU PUT IN THE NEWS ON PAGE FIVE IN BIG LETTERS. MRS. PARSONS DOING FINE THANKS TO MR. JONES. AND PUT THE LICENSE NUMBER OF YOUR CAR SO WE WILL KNOW YOUR CAR. NO EXCITEMENT AS YOU WIFE CANT STAND IT. GO TO THE DAILY MIRROR AND INSERT THAT WITH OUR CAR NUMBER AND EVERYTHING WILL BE FINE FOR ALL HANDS.

THE PAPER IS THE DAILY NEWS PAGE FIVT TILL YOU HEAR FORM ME

MR. PAUL JONES.

In a letter to the FBI's technical laboratory in Washington, D.C., Inspector E.J. Connelley requested that the original letter from Paul Jones be examined for latent fingerprints and also requested that they attempt to determine the make and model of the typewriter used to create the letter. He went on to state that the writer of this letter had requested that an ad be placed, in big letters, on page five of the *New York Daily News*. Inspector Connelley believed that this would be impractical at the time due to the fact that it would have been necessary to make special arrangements with the newspaper in order to insert such an ad with special type requirements. The ad itself, which mentions the Parsons name, would result in publicity that would prevent any successful attempt to apprehend the writer.

Connelley showed the letter to William Parsons and explained that he was somewhat skeptical as to the letter's authenticity. He also explained his reasoning in not following the instructions of the letter writer. He did state however that a future letter from this individual might provide a means of contact that would not result in mass publicity.

All during the early part of July, the tension among members of the McDonell and Parsons families had grown. Many family members now held the belief that Anna Kupryanova was responsible for Alice's disappearance. William's brother-in-law Richardson Pratt had informed Inspector Connelley that he was contemplating making arrangements to have William Parsons's mental stability examined. Both John and Bunny Parsons had discussed the possibility that William had killed Alice in a fit of rage. To compound matters, William told his sister Laura Pratt that he was in love with Anna Kupryanova. This information moved quickly through the family and eventually reached the ears of Molly Parsons and Bessie Williams, both of whom were now living at Long Meadow Farm. The turbulent family emotions, compounded by their heightened suspicions of both William and Anna, were further exacerbated by the endless press inquiries regarding Willian and Anna's personal relationship. All of this led to the decision that Anna Kupryanova should move out of the Stony Brook home. So, on July 16, Anna moved out of Long Meadow Farm and moved into the YWCA in New York City, and young Roy Parsons was sent to the Society of St. Johnland's live-in summer camp for boys in Kings Park.

Anna was extremely unhappy with her new housing situation and endeavored to change her living conditions by further manipulating William Parsons. Shortly after she arrived at the YWCA, she advised William during one of his visits that she was being annoyed by numerous suitors who wished to marry her; that they had been sending her flowers; that one had been offering her money and bonds if she would marry him; and one had specifically offered her a gift of $50,000 in bonds should she agree to marry him. Anna followed up her claims with a letter to William the very next day. Her letter was intercepted and copied by the FBI. It read as follows:

I felt much better after seeing you yesterday. I know now that the worst is over and you will be strong and know you own mind. I will see you on Thursday and will tell you all about it. In the meantime try to get rid of B. You will feel much better. It was a great mistake in the first place to let her come. I hope you will understand my letter.

Anna's reference to B was in regard to Bessie Williams, who was still residing at Long Meadow Farm. Anna's actions, and the results of her actions, were indicative of the tremendous influence she maintained over William Parsons and the ease with which she could manipulate him. William believed every word Anna had to say regarding her suitors and acted quickly to move her to a new location.

To the surprise of many people involved with the investigation, another letter from the purported kidnappers arrived a week later. This one was addressed to Anna Kupryanova's friend Mrs. Matislav Golovan at 40-28 195th Street, Flushing. A note written on the outside of the envelope read, "Please deliver this to Anna Kupryanova personally at the earliest possible moment." The letter was handwritten in green ink and had been mailed on July 14 from Elizabeth, New Jersey. The letter was as follows:

July 14, 1937
Dear Anna

This is from a heartbroken woman who was forced into a most unhappy thing. My heart bleeds for you and yours. As long as Mrs. Parson does not return everyone and the papers will make you and your family also unhappy by their false suspicion. I have brought myself to this decision. The thing must end sometime. In 48 hours there will be found in one of the outhouses a sheet of paper with the same as the one enclosed. The exact location of Alice Parsons' body. I have a way putting a note there. Do not try to trap me. I am trying to help you. May god bless you and forgive a most unhappy woman.
Mary

The letter from "Mary" was followed three later by another handwritten letter in green ink. It too was mailed to Mrs. Golovan and marked to the attention of Anna. The letter read as follows:

July 17, 1937
Dear Mrs. Kupryanova

I am sorry I could not do as I promised in my letter from Elizabeth, N.J. The officers and others were so active around the place it was unsafe. When the body of Mrs. Parsons is found where he put it I know all will be clear. Those who have been unfair will then think of the harm it might have done. Why don't the papers leave you alone. Please believe me, most unhappy woman, when I say I was forced into what I did. I did not believe they would go so far. The only safe thing for me to do is to mail you or Mr. Parsons a document showing the exact location of the body of Alice. I will show the roads and the spot. It may take me a little time to prepare this as I am not familiar with the place. Very soon I will send the diagram to you or Mr. Parsons. God bless you and yours. You will never hear from me again. I am going away.

Mary

The paper will show who I am.

On Wednesday, July 21, 1937, Anna's attorney Benjamin Shiverts mailed both letters to the FBI's New York office. The very next day, William Parsons engaged Isaac Levy of New York City as his attorney. William had borrowed $5,000 from his sister Laura Pratt with the understanding that none of the money could be used for Anna's defense. Over the next several days, William, Mr. Levy, Anna and her attorney Mr. Shiverts met numerous times.

On Saturday, July 24, 1937, Anna Kupryanova received a third letter from Mary. It was addressed to Anna Cooper and delivered to her at the YWCA. The envelope bore two three-cent stamps. The mailing address on the envelope was typewritten; the letter itself, however, was in the same handwriting as the previous letters and written in the same green ink. It had been mailed from New Jersey just like the previous "Mary" letters.

In this ten-page letter, Mary explained that Alice had died from pneumonia on July 9 and that the pneumonia was due to exposure. She went on to say that she and her brother had a falling out as a result of Alice's death and that her brother had left her. Mary stated that she was in failing health and intended to sail to Europe soon, but before going, she would send Bill, at some later point, some token of Alice. She also indicated that she and her brother had friends in New Jersey, which is why the letters had been mailed from there. She went on to write that both she and her brother were Long Island people. The letter contained considerably detailed information regarding the dress that Alice had supposedly been wearing. Mary indicated that she could not send Alice's dress but did describe it in detail, indicating that the dress closed from left to right rather than from the right to left as would be the usual situation in the front of a woman's dress. She said it had three buttons. In fact, Anna recalled that the dress Mary described had been given to Alice by her sister-in-law Laura Pratt primarily because Alice was left-handed. This information, when examined in light of the previous three letters, pointed to the fact that Paul and Mary Jones were siblings, and there was an ever-growing possibility that they may have been the couple in the car that drove Alice away from Long Meadow Farm on June 9.

The day after receiving Mary's letter, Anna purchased a large envelope and mailed this multipage letter to her attorney Benjamin Shiverts. The envelope was mailed from Farmingdale, Long Island. She also mailed two other letters that day. One was an additional letter to Shiverts regarding her son, and the other was a letter so someone she knew in Russia.

William had been working studiously with the YWCA to find new accommodations for Anna. Finally, arrangements were made to place Anna at the home of Russian Baroness de Gasser and Mrs. F.W. Merritt, on Merritt Road, Farmingdale. John and Bunny Parsons provided Anna with transportation and assistance in moving her belongings to her new residence. It appeared that all involved with this move had agreed to refer to Anna as Anna Cooper. Neither the baroness nor Mrs. Merritt was told that Anna was the woman currently in the headlines of every major newspaper in New York, Los Angeles and Chicago. Anna's move to the home on Merritt Road worked to the benefit of the FBI. The home itself was easy to surveil, and the bureau immediately tapped the telephone line. Unfortunately for Anna, the Baroness de Gasser would not turn a blind eye to what she considered improper late-night visits to Anna by an unidentified man, and tensions in this home soon began to grow.

On August 7, 1937, a fifth letter from the suspected kidnappers was received. This one had been mailed from Salem, New Jersey, and was sent directly to the FBI's New York office. This letter was from Paul Jones and had been prepared on a similar typewriter as the first letter, with all words being in capital letters. The letter from Paul read as follows:

G MEN AND COPS

IN JULY I COMMUNICATED WITH WILLIAM PARSONS TO FURNISH ME $40,000 FOR THE RETURN OF HIS WIFE AND TO COVER THE GREAT EXPENSE I HAD BEING ONLY A GUARD THINGS MOVED FAST PARSONS DID NOT ANSWER HIS WIFE DIED THEN MY SISTER IN HER WEAKNESS WROTE TO THE RUSSIAN WOMAN GIVING HER THE LOCATION OF THE BODY OF ALICE PARSONS

I HAVE WATCHED THE PAPERS CAREFULLY BUT YOU HAVE KEPT FROM THE PUBLIC THE FINDING OF THE BODY THIS WILL NOT CATCH US   F GO AHEAD IN IN YOUR DUMB WAY

I KNEW YOU WERE IN THE THING FROM THE START AND ALL MY PLANS WERE MADE WITH THIS THOUGHT AND YOU WOULD NOT HAVE CAUGHT ME WITH ALL YOUR SMARTNESS

I DO NOT WRITE YOU TO PLAGUE YOU MY ONLY THOUGHT IS TO PROTECT MARY SHE WAS NOT A WILLING PARTY TO ANYTHING AND DID NOT KNOW OR EXPECT THE END IT WILL BE BEST FOR PARSON TO SEE SHE IS PROTECTED OR ELSE IF HE DOES THIS EVERTHING WILL N BE FINE FOR ALL HANDS

MR PAUL JONES

This letter and its contents were discussed with both William and Anna. Anna appeared to be very impressed with this particular letter and was also impressed with the fact that it appeared to confirm everyone's suspicions that Paul and Mary Jones were siblings. When the discussion returned to the most recent "Mary" letter, Anna reiterated that Mary never discussed whether or not Alice had received a proper burial.

Anna Kupryanova continued to have a difficult time at Baroness de Gasser's home in Farmingdale. During the first week in August, Anna admitted her identity to the baroness. This upset the baroness to such an extent that she called her parish priest and said to him that she was in terrible trouble and needed to see him immediately. After meeting with her priest, the baroness was convinced that the relationship between

Anna and William was improper in view of the very recent and suspicious disappearance of Williams's wife. The baroness then told Anna that William Parsons was not to visit her at the house in the future. This upset Anna greatly, and on the morning of August 9, Anna decided to leave the house. She telephoned Bunny Parsons and asked that she come to Farmingdale at once to pick her up. Her second call was to William at the farmhouse. Anna explained the situation to him and told him that Bunny was on the way to get her. William indicated that he too would come to Farmingdale right away.

John Parsons, his wife and William Parsons all arrived at Anna's Farmingdale home in the early afternoon. Anna's belongings were packed into John Parsons's car while Anna was driven to Bayside in William's car. William was now in a difficult position. His attorney had already advised him that it would be best if he did not reside with Anna, at least until the investigation was over. Both his sister Molly and Bessie Williams were adamant in their position that Anna not return to the farm. In addition, William had very little income with which to both keep the farm running and pay rent for a place for Anna to live. William had already tried to borrow money from Bessie Williams and had been turned down.

With all of these factors in mind, William approached John and Bunny Parsons with a proposal. William suggested to Bunny that she accept Anna as a housekeeper and nursemaid for their new baby and pay her forty dollars per month. In William's mind, this solution would provide a rent-free place for Anna and Roy to stay and, at the same time, provide for additional income. Bunny Parsons quickly put an end to William's proposal. She would later relate to the FBI that she would never have trusted Anna Kupryanova with her child and that she believed that Anna may actually have had plans to do away with William at some point in the future.

That evening, after having his proposal rebuffed by his brother, William decided that Anna would return to Long Meadow Farm in three days. When he arrived back at his home, he informed Bessie Williams that it was his intention to have Anna move back into the house and that he hoped that she and Molly would remain. It was his desire that all of the family members in the household would remain peaceful and harmonious after Anna's return. Miss Williams stated emphatically to William that she had no intention of staying in the same house as Anna and continued with harsh comments regarding Anna's character. William responded by saying that Anna should not be judged and that "the G-men have done nothing but try to fix the blame on Anna and me."

Unbeknownst to both William and Anna, their every movement was being watched by the FBI. Every time Anna shifted living quarters, she was followed by a surveillance team of FBI agents ready to install new listening devices and wiretaps wherever she happened to be. Even their family outings were surveilled. One such outing had William and Anna picking up Roy from his camp in Kings Park and taking him to a beach in an eastern Long Island village known as Wainscott. Their every move and every stop were marked and monitored by a FBI surveillance team. Every time William pulled his car to the side of the road, the location was marked and later searched thoroughly for anything that might have been discarded on the ground. The FBI's surveillance team followed them all along Route 27 on the south shore of Long Island and through sleepy little villages like Hampton Bays. Once William and Anna's long day at the beach ended, they were followed home.

William Parsons's efforts to have Anna return to Long Meadow Farm were finally put to rest by his own attorney, Isaac Levy. Levy pointedly told William that if Anna returned to William's home, he would no longer represent him. He also reiterated his previous advice that William should keep a distance from Anna Kupryanova while the investigation was still ongoing. The very next day, William located furnished rooms for Anna at 35-14 Parsons Boulevard, Flushing. It was now William's plan to live with his brother John and visit Anna every day. John Parsons, in what he claimed was an effort to help his brother, told him that he disapproved of the relationship that William had with Anna and his outward show of affection for her. These comments caused a major falling-out between the brothers, with William finally calling John "another one of those god-dammed Pratts." William then, in a breach of trust with his sister Laura, contacted his attorney Levy and told him to take half of the $5,000 retainer and use it to pay for Anna's legal fees. William packed up his things that evening and joined Anna at the Parsons Boulevard rooming house.

The FBI had been waiting for him. They had already secured a room directly adjacent to Anna's room that included a connecting locked door. A microphone was quickly installed at the door, and the telephone line was in the process of being tapped.

On August 16, a sixth letter arrived. Because of the contents of the envelope, it was believed that the letter had been sent by Mary Jones. It had been mailed to John Parsons, Gables, Bayside, L.I., N.Y. The letter had been placed in a small, heavy brown manila envelope and the envelope sealed with six three-cent stamps over the flap. The front of the envelope contained a three-cent stamp and a ten-cent stamp. It had been postmarked at 7:00 a.m., August 16, 1937, at Station F, New York.

John Parsons suspected that the unopened letter was in regard to Alice's kidnapping, and he contacted Inspector Connelley immediately. When Connelly arrived at John's home, he took immediate possession of the envelope. John Parsons commented on the fact that the address on the envelope read "Gables" and indicated that he did not know how anyone not connected with the case would be aware of his home address since he was not listed in the telephone book. The envelope was carefully handled and examined by Inspector Connelley. It contained two sheets of paper with letters that had been cut from a newspaper. The letter read as follows:

> *Sorry delay. Alice Died pneumonia. Brother responsible kidnaped. Body destroyed complete.*

The word *body* was written "Bodi" and the I was retraced in green ink to make it a Y. The last word, *complete*, is in handwriting and appears to have been cut out of a letter. With this letter was another piece of paper to which was attached a small gold pin with a gold backing and a white face. The pin contained four pearls and four blue sapphires. Bunny Parsons immediately identified it as a pin belonging to Alice.

The next evening, Bunny Parsons telephoned Anna at her rooming house. The call was intercepted and recorded by the FBI. During the call, Bunny told Anna about the receipt of the letter the previous day. Anna acted quite surprised at the news of a new letter and stated that she would come straight to Bunny's home.

After picking up the letter from John Parsons, Inspector Connelley drove out to Long Meadow Farm, where he met with William Parsons. William, Molly Parsons and Bessie Williams were each shown the piece of jewelry sent by the kidnappers. William at first stated that he was certain that the pin had belonged to Alice. However, Molly and Bessie indicated that they did not recognize it and were doubtful that it belonged to Alice. With that said, the amenable William quickly changed his opinion and became suddenly doubtful about its identification.

The next afternoon, August 18, 1937, Inspector Connelley and Special Agent H.G. Robinson arrived at the law office of Benjamin Shiverts at 61 Broadway, New York City. Connelley had arranged to have a meeting with Anna Kupryanova and her lawyer to discuss the new letter and the jewelry that had been enclosed in the envelope. At that meeting, Anna positively identified the pin as having belonged to Alice. Anna stated that at one time one of the pearls had come loose when the dress was placed into the wash with the pin still attached, and the pearl had been reattached to the pin with glue. Anna also said that Alice had two very small bar pins with the same kind of sapphire stones in them that matched the circular pin. The bar pins were used in pinning the cuffs or sleeves of her dress. Connelley was very pleased with this identification. He now had three positive identifications of the jewelry and knew that the letter writer had been in contact, at some point, with Alice Parsons.

Over the next ten days, William and Anna spent most of their time together at the rooming house under the watchful eyes and ears of the FBI surveillance teams. In one of their more revealing recorded conversations, William told Anna that the period of time since Alice's disappearance had been three months of happiness and bliss. He asked Anna why they could not have six years more. He also stated that they should not wait the expected seven years in order to get married and that he wanted to marry Anna within the next year. He then said, "I think I will shake the dust of this country off my feet and we will go to Europe."

Many of William and Anna's recorded conversations during this period focused on the settlement of Alice's estate. It became clear to them that, without a body, Alice could not be declared legally dead, and neither he, Anna nor Roy would be able to collect their inheritance from Alice's substantial estate. Anna, on several occasions, indicated that it would be best for all if Alice's body was found. In William's conversations with his attorney regarding Alice's estate, he was advised that it would be impossible at this time to receive any monies from the estate and that the matter of the settlement would have to be held in abeyance, possibly for seven years. The attorney went on to tell William that the waiting time could even be further extended by some members of Alice's family who might wish to contest the settlement of her estate even after she was declared legally dead.

As William and Anna were planning their future together, Alice's family members were making plans to disrupt that future. Alice's brother Frank McDonell and her aunt Bessie Williams were now convinced that William and Anna had murdered Alice. They sent William a letter informing him that they were attempting to have a new conservator appointed for Alice's estate. Their plan was to remove William as conservator and tie up Alice's estate for as long as possible in order to leave William with no funds. With Alice's half-ownership of the farm and Bessie Williams holding the mortgage, there was little chance that William would receive any large sums from the sale of the farm. In addition, any inheritance due Alice from Colonel Williams's estate would take years to recover without Alice being declared legally dead. Alice's family believed, as did the FBI, that the moment William ran out of money, Anna Kupryanova would leave him and find another source of sustenance for her and her child. Separating William from Anna was paramount in their minds. They were convinced that once Anna rejected William, he would then cease protecting her and reveal what he knew regarding Alice's disappearance.

Inspector Connelley was supportive of Alice's family's efforts to thwart William Parsons's financial stability. Connelley was of the belief that every means of pressure possible should be brought down on William and Anna in order to locate Alice Parsons. In a telephone conversation with Director Hoover, Connelley stated that there were two good microphones in the boardinghouse room occupied by William and Anna and that the surveillance team was getting a lot of good information. He told Hoover that it was clear from the recorded conversations that Anna knew the location of Alice's body but would not tell William for fear that he would break down.

On the last day of August, Anna and Roy moved into a new apartment at 40-10 Corporal Kennedy Street, Bayside, New York. William Parsons rented the apartment and introduced Anna as his sister. William, who had been previously dividing his overnight hours among the farm, John's home and Anna's furnished room, now moved in with Anna. Parsons then transferred all of Anna's money into his own account and began moving the home furnishings from the farm to the new apartment. He then began to sell all of the livestock and equipment at Long Meadow Farm. The FBI was well aware of these activities and moved surveillance teams and equipment into a first-floor storage room at the Corporal Kennedy Street address. They then installed new microphones in William and Anna's apartment. It was through this surveillance that Inspector Connelley learned of William Parsons's upcoming trip to California.

Six days later, another letter arrived. This was the seventh letter received from the Jones family and the fifth letter received from Mary. The letter arrived at Stony Brook on the morning of September 7. This letter, like the last from Mary, was short. The letter read:

> *This may not be right. If better information found later I will send another diagram. I was not present when body was buried. I hope this well end all you worry. God bless you.*
> *Mary*

Enclosed with the letter was a roughly drawn map of the roads in and around the Parsons farmhouse and a location marked where Alice's body could be found. Numerous FBI agents immediately assembled at the farm and began a search based on the roughly drawn map. After hours of searching, it was reported that nothing had been found. Inspector Connelley met with both William and Anna to discuss this most recent letter and the hand-drawn diagram that it contained. He would contact them both again a few days later to let them know that the FBI's technical laboratory had recovered a latent fingerprint from the letter.

Seven days later, on September 14, 1937, a story appeared in the afternoon edition of the *New York Journal American*. A *Journal American* reporter by the name of McCollum wrote that William Parsons and Anna Kupryanova had been receiving letters from a person known as Mary. He reported that Mary and her brother may have been responsible for Alice Parsons's kidnapping and might know the location of her buried body. This was the first time it had been reported in the press that Alice Parsons might have died in captivity. The story went on further to state that a close family member reported that a brooch or pin had been sent in one of the letters to William Parsons and that the ransom had been increased from $25,000 to $40,000. When contacted prior to the story's publication, Anna's attorney Benjamin Shiverts confirmed the existence of the letters and the positive identification of Alice's brooch. Shiverts stated that it was very unfortunate that the existence of the letters was disclosed but indicated that since the press already knew of them, he would have to confirm the fact that they had been received. When contacted by the press, the New York office of the FBI would make no comment.

Later that evening, Basil Gallagher, a reporter for the *New York Post*, interviewed John Parsons at his Bayside home. John also confirmed the receipt of the various letters and the brooch in question. There was much discussion among both the FBI officials and various family members as to who leaked the information to the press. It was noted at the time that McCollum, who had broken the story, was the reporter for the *New York Journal American* who had been stationed during business hours at the office of Richardson Pratt at 30 Rockefeller Plaza in New York City. Later interviews of William Parsons and Anna Kupryanova indicated that they did not release this information to the press. This was further verified by the FBI's recordings of conversations that took place in William and Anna's apartment.

Just hours before the story broke in the *New York Journal American*, Inspector Connelley reached out to Assistant District Attorney Lindsay Henry. He advised him that the newspapers were about to publish a story that there had been letters received that indicated a willingness on the part of some person to disclose the location of Alice's body. He said that the FBI was not prepared to verify the authenticity of these letters but had been going along with the situation in the hope that a communication would eventually be received that disclosed the location of Alice Parsons's body. Henry indicated that this was a good idea and that he would avoid any comments to the press about the existence of these letters and would communicate this information to District Attorney Hill. In the end, most of the publicity surrounding these letters focused on their content and not the FBI's assessment of their authenticity or their value to the investigation.

The eighth and final letter came from Mary Jones and arrived at Stony Brook on the morning of September 16, 1937. It was addressed to William Parsons and had been mailed the day before from the Hudson Terminal in New York City. The letter read as follows:

> *I have tried to help you and your housekeeper, believing the finger of suspicion unjustly pointed to you. I wished to trust in and help you. However Mrs. Kupryanova for some reason at this time has unwisely and contrary to my wishes given information to the officers and the papers.*
>
> *My heart aches. I cannot rest. I worry over poor Mrs. Parsons uncared for. I am trying to get to you the information so she may have a Christian burial and attention. When my mission has been accomplished or the matter is ended in other ways I will leave forever. They may check New Jersey. I do not worry. Bless you.*
> *Mary*

On the evening of September 16, Inspector Connelley visited William and Anna at their Corporal Kennedy Street apartment. During separate interviews, William stated he was very impressed with the information being provided by the writer and believed that Mary would continue to write and would eventually send the location of Alice's body.

Inspector Connelley then discussed the letter with Anna Kupryanova. Connelley offered the opinion that the person calling herself Mary was mentally unstable and might even be just some crazy person writing letters who had no intention of disclosing where Alice's body was located. Anna quickly jumped to Mary's defense and indicated that she believed Mary to be a very smart woman and was satisfied that she would eventually disclose to them the location of the body. Anna referred to the fact that Mary must have worn gloves when writing the letters, with the exception of the one letter with a fingerprint, which was sent with the diagram on September 7. Connelley suggested that Mary may have gained the impression, based upon the recent press releases, that Anna had violated her trust and had supplied information to the press about her letters. Anna disagreed and remained convinced that Mary would continue to communicate with them.

Once Inspector Connelley, William and Anna had finished discussing the most recent letter from Mary, William began to tell Connelley about his future plans. William said that he was leaving New York on September 26 for California with his sister Laura Pratt. In later discussions with Laura Pratt the FBI learned that the Pratts were financing William's trip to California with the goal of separating him from Anna for a short time, during which Laura might be able to convince him to tell what he knew about Alice's disappearance.

William and his sister would be traveling by train with a stop in Chicago. William indicated that he would be shipping his automobile by boat in the next few days and it should arrive there on approximately the same day as his train arrived. He then said that it was his plan to have Anna and Roy join him later in California, with the possibility of all of them relocating to Canada at some point.

11

THE CONNELLEY GAMBIT

The letters received from Paul and Mary Jones had played a major role in the investigation of Alice Parsons's disappearance. To this day, press articles, books and stories regarding Alice Parsons's disappearance still refer to the "Mary Jones" letters and how the information in those letters affected the investigation. What is important to note about this critical part of the investigation, however, is that the letters received from Paul and Mary Jones were nothing more than an FBI ruse. It was a ruse that ultimately transformed into a mental chess game between Inspector E.J. Connelley and Anna Kupryanova.

The very first letter, received on July 8, 1937, was a Special Delivery letter addressed to Mr. William H. Parsons, Stony Brook, Long Island. It had been sent by a Paul Jones. The FBI determined early on that Mr. Jones was nothing more than a con man and extortionist who was attempting to capitalize on the Parsons family's misfortune.

His sister, Mary Jones, existed in one place and in one place only. She existed in the mind of her creator, Inspector E.J. Connelley. Inspector Connelley dictated each of the so-called Mary letters to an FBI stenographer in the New York office who, using Connelley's own signature green ink pen, would create each Mary Jones letter. It was the same green ink pen that Inspector Connelley used to sign each of his reports to Director J. Edgar Hoover. The purpose of sending these letters was to provide a circumstance in which Anna and/or William would be induced to provide the location of Alice Parsons's body. Connelley believed that such a circumstance would assist William Parsons in his efforts to collect the inheritance from Alice's estate without having to wait seven more years for her to be declared legally dead.

The July 14 and July 17 letters were both addressed to Anna Kupryanova. Both letters contained additional blank sheets of writing paper. It was Connelley's hope that Anna would use these sheets at some point in the future. To ensure their future identification, Connelley had placed Murine markings on each blank sheet that were barely visible to the naked eye but could be easily seen under ultraviolet light. Anna had delivered both letters to her attorney Benjamin Shiverts shortly after she received them. Her attorney promptly mailed them to Inspector Connelley. When Connelley received the letters, he immediately noted that the blank pieces of writing paper were missing.

The July 24 ten-page letter from Mary, which Anna claimed had been delivered to her at the YWCA, was a complete figment of Anna Kupryanova's imagination. Anna claimed that the letter stated that Alice had died from pneumonia on July 9 and that the pneumonia had been brought on by exposure. Anna also claimed that the letter indicated that Alice received a proper burial. Anna would later change her story on this one fact. Proof that such a letter never existed can be found in the simple fact that Inspector Connelley, who was in fact Mary, never sent such a letter. Anna also claimed that she had purchased a large envelope and mailed this multipage letter to her attorney Benjamin Shiverts on the Sunday after she received the letter. Anna had spent that entire Sunday with John and Molly Parsons, and they had no recollection of Anna mailing a letter that day. Additionally, Shiverts informed the FBI that he never received the letter. When questioned, Anna claimed that it must have been lost in the mail. This event was followed by an effort on the part of Inspector Connelley to spur Anna Kupryanova to write her own letter and add credibility to his ruse. Toward this effort, Inspector Connelley placed advertisements in each of the New York daily papers on July 28, 29 and 30, requesting that Mary and Paul Jones communicate with William Parsons or Anna Kupryanova.

The fifth letter in this sophisticated ruse was sent directly to the FBI's New York office on August 7. This letter was reportedly from Paul Jones and indicated an increase in the ransom demand from $25,000 to $40,000. Inspector Connelley had had the FBI's technical laboratory identify the manufacture of the typewriter used in the original Paul Jones extortion letter. He then used a similar typewriter to create a new letter that closely matched the format of the Paul Jones original.

On August 16, a sixth letter was sent to John and Molly Parsons's home. It had been postmarked at 7:00 a.m., August 16, 1937, at Station F, New York. In this short letter from Mary Jones, she claimed that her brother was responsible for the kidnapping and that Alice's body had been completely destroyed. Enclosed with the letter was a brooch that had reportedly belonged to Alice Parsons. The brooch was pinned to a blank page of writing paper. The blank page was actually one of the Murine-marked blank pages that had been inserted into the letters from Mary on July 14 and July 17 that had been sent to Anna Kupryanova.

As Inspector Connelley had hoped, Anna had removed the blank pages and used them in her effort to assume the persona of Mary.

The seventh letter arrived at Long Meadow Farm on September 7. The eighth letter arrived a week later. Both of these letters were from Mary Jones and had again been created by Inspector E.J. Connelley in his signature green ink. The letter of September 7 contained a roughly drawn map of the roads in and around the Parsons farm and a location marked where Alice's body could be found. The letter indicated that Mary was not absolutely sure of the location. Connelley had hoped that Anna would seize on this opportunity to again assume the persona of Mary and send a more precise map with the location of Alice's body. In order to help convince William and Anna of the FBI's belief in the words of Mary Jones, Connelley ordered numerous FBI agents to immediately assemble at the farm and begin a search based on the roughly drawn map contained in Mary's letter. He also convinced William and Anna that a fingerprint had been found on the letter.

The letter of September 16 targeted William Parsons and suggested that Alice's body could have been found if it were not for the actions of Anna. Connelley had now placed William and Anna in a position where they needed to weigh the risk of prosecution over the risk of financial stability. Should Anna reveal where the body was, even through the persona of Mary Jones, she and William could still face a murder prosecution. Anna had to decide if the letters from Paul and Mary provided enough evidence to prove their guilt and would be enough to keep her and William out of prison. Anna also knew that if she chose to identify where Alice's body was located, she and William would be able to collect the inheritance from Alice's estate. In the end, Anna returned to her own prior words of advice: "If there is no body, there is no murder."

12

LEAVING TOWN

On September 17, 1937, William Parsons's attorney Isaac Levy telephoned Inspector Connelley at his New York office. During the conversation, Levy informed Connelley that William Parsons was planning to issue a press release in three days. The press release would be a plea to the mysterious persons who had been sending in the letters and would specifically ask them to reveal the location of Alice's body.

William Parsons was under a great deal of pressure during this mid-September period. In addition to the planned press release, he was making every effort to put his financial affairs in order before his upcoming trip to California. One of his biggest financial obstacles was the sale of Long Meadow Farm. It would be difficult if not impossible for him to sell the farm while his wife was missing due to the fact that Alice's name was on the title to the property. William was also in desperate need of an extension on the $6,000 mortgage held by Bessie Williams. Bessie was not inclined to do this for William, which left the possibility of a foreclosure in the near future. Although he had a buyer willing to pay him $13,000 for the farm, he had to settle for a rental agreement paying him $600 per year for seven years with any rents paid to be applied against the purchase price.

On September 18, 1937, Alice Parsons's brother Frank McDonell telephoned Inspector Connelley to discuss the issue of Alice's conservatorship. He indicated that William Parsons had agreed to sign a waiver of his right as first choice to be conservator. The document was currently being drafted by the law firm of Cullen and Dyckman.

This was an important step, as Alice's estate was to receive $20,000 in the next few weeks from the estate of her uncle Colonel Timothy Williams. Alice's aunt Bessie Williams was the administrator for that estate and would be delaying the payment until she was assured that there was no possibility of William Parsons obtaining control of that money. Frank McDonell told the inspector that in a recent discussion with William Parsons, he had informed William that even after seven years he, and his brother, Howard, would vigorously contest the adjudication of Alice's estate or the probate of her will. Frank and Howard impressed this upon William so that he would realize the futility of expecting any money from Alice's estate even after seven years.

Two days later, William's attorney Isaac Levy contacted various members of the New York press. They gathered in his office at 70 Pine Street in lower Manhattan, and each was given a copy of William Parsons's statement. It read as follows:

> *I am satisfied from the letters that I have received that my wife is no more. The writer of these letters seems very anxious to relieve my distress. It is a cruel thing to keep me in suspense. Whoever it is that seems to have knowledge of the whereabouts of my wife's body can have no realization of what it would mean to be able to give my wife proper burial.*
>
> *What has occurred has done so much to wreck my life that I find it absolutely necessary to leave the scene of this sad tragedy. I am preparing to dispose of my home at Stony Brook and I plan to find activity in some other part of the country. I shall, however, not give up hope that the persons who have knowledge of where my wife's body may be found will give me the little comfort of being permitted to give my wife proper burial.*

There were several follow-up questions from the press. Much of the focus appeared to be on the identification of the brooch that had been mailed to William from the kidnappers. William Parsons told them that it was a family heirloom worth approximately fifty dollars. William indicated that although he could not specifically remember seeing Alice wear this piece of jewelry, it had been identified by other family members.

During the third week in September, William, Anna and Roy were at Long Meadow Farm preparing it for closure. They spent three days moving personal items from the farmhouse to their apartment. On their final day there, a van arrived from the Bayside Van Storage Company and removed the final pieces of furniture from the Parsons farmhouse.

All during this period, William and Anna's movements were closely monitored by the FBI. While at the farm, their activities were also being noted by Gus Alton, the farm's new caretaker hired by Laura Pratt. Each time they returned to the apartment, their conversations were monitored and recorded by the FBI surveillance team sitting just down the hall in a storage room. One of these recorded conversations indicated that there had been a considerable argument between William and Anna over William's failure to positively identify the brooch that had been received in the mail from Mary Jones. William had responded by saying that he would have been more certain of the identification if he had known that Anna had definitely identified it. The recorded conversations also revealed details of William's travel plans to California. It appeared that he and his sister Laura Pratt would be traveling together to Los Angeles, where they would be staying at the Savoy Hotel. They would then proceed to the home of their brother Oliver Parsons in Carpinteria, California.

On September 22, 1937, Anna Kupryanova went on the offensive. Her attorney Benjamin Shiverts had arranged for a press conference that was to be held in his office at 61 Broadway in New York City. Anna made a lengthy statement to the press to the effect that the G-Men had silenced her and she had always been willing to discuss the case. She claimed she had nothing to hide and never felt under suspicion. In a message directed at the letter writer Mary Jones, Anna said, "Since she appears to be a religious woman, I want to ask her on her honor to keep her promise to tell me everything in connection with the case. We do not seek to punish. We only want information about the disposal of the body." She went on to tell the press that she believed the letter writers were the man and woman who had taken Alice Parsons away from the farm on June 9, 1937. She then lied to the press by telling them she was living in Manhattan. Photographs were taken at the press conference, and the following day, the story and Anna Kupryanova's photograph appeared in all of the major New York newspapers. Recorded conversations indicated that Anna was quite pleased with her press coverage. It motivated her to call another press interview two days later.

Benjamin Shiverts arranged for Anna to meet with *New York Post* reporters Maureen McKernan and Basil Gallagher. The interview lasted three hours. During the interview, Anna said that a new note, the eighth from Mary and Paul Jones, had been received within the past few days. She claimed to have given the authorities detailed descriptions of the kidnappers and provided those descriptions to the reporters during the interview. She went on to state that the investigation of Alice's disappearance had been badly mishandled due to the lack of cooperation between the local and federal authorities. She claimed that she and William Parsons had been accused of all manner of crimes by the G-Men and local authorities and subjected to interrogations "too horrid to talk about."

She went on to state that the G-Men had shut her away from everybody and would not let either her or William Parsons answer any questions and that the police ransacked the house when they arrived on June 9.

During the interview, Anna was asked if she had written the ransom note found in Alice's car on the night of June 9. Anna denied the accusation, and her attorney was quoted: "Suffolk County District Attorney L. Barron Hill had denied that a handwriting expert had identified the kidnap note writing as Anna Kupryanova's—in spite of assertions to the contrary." Anna further declared:

> *The police left no doubt that they suspect us of doing away with Mrs. Parsons. Some of the things they did to us are too horrible to describe. Once the G-Men took me to New York with Mr. Parsons. For three days they gave us a third degree. For three days I was not allowed to sleep. They kept me sitting up straight in a chair answering questions. They did not touch us but it was a awful ordeal. We also submitted to a lie detector test voluntarily. Apparently they were satisfied we told the truth because we heard no more about it. They tried all the methods to break us that you read about in dime novels.*

Anna went on to explain the receipt of the various letters from Paul and Mary Jones and provided details to the reporters regarding the letters' contents. In a stinging blow to the FBI, Anna stated that she believed that the letters were entirely authentic, and had the letters been handled properly, the person responsible for Alice Parsons's disappearance might have been caught. Anna was also quoted as saying that the mysterious people who had been writing indicated that they were Long Island people and that they undoubtedly read in the papers about Alice's inheritance and that this answered the question why Alice Parsons had been targeted for a kidnapping. Anna also claimed that Paul and Mary Jones were familiar with the obscure roads behind Long Meadow Farm and had named the roads in one of the letters. Most of Anna's statements were untrue, of course. The last time there had been any mention of Alice Parsons's inheritance in a daily newspaper was seven years prior, and no roads "behind" the farm had been named in the letters. Anna Kupryanova ended her *New York Post* interview by telling the reporters two additional lies. She told them that she was not living with William Parsons at that time and that she had no intention of going away with him.

The following day, William Parsons read Anna's statements in the *New York Post* and, in a recorded conversation, severely criticized her for the comments she made regarding the FBI. Anna responded by lying to William and telling him that the comments in the *New York Post* article had been made by her attorney and not her. It was apparent from further conversations that day that Anna was elated over the success of her publicity campaign and had taken particular delight in the pictures of herself that had appeared in the newspapers. It was apparent that she had started a scrapbook collection of these items and would take them out and review them from time to time. At one point, she indicated that, due to her newfound popularity, she might insist on reporters paying her for future interviews. William Parsons asked her to promise him that she would not do any more interviews. She indicated that she would make no such promise.

Later that evening, two *New York News* reporters showed up at the door of William and Anna's apartment. They requested an interview with Anna but were refused. Anna indicated that any interview would need to be arranged through her attorney. The reporters, being suspicious as to William's presence in the apartment, had asked him if he was living there. William claimed that the apartment belonged to Anna and, in explaining his presence, stated that he had just brought some things from the Stony Brook farmhouse. Once the reporters left, William quickly packed an overnight bag and proceeded to the home of his brother John Parsons in Bayside. Both William and Anna were quite upset over the fact that their apartment had been located by the press. William was well aware of the fact that the press knew his car, and from that night forward he parked his car several blocks from the apartment and walked the rest of the distance. The FBI's recording log ended that evening with a note that said, "Illicit relations occurred as between Anna and William Parsons prior to his departure for the home of John Parsons where he slept the night of September 26, 1937."

On September 27, 1937, Inspector Connelley interviewed Anna Kupryanova regarding the numerous misstatements that appeared in her immigration application and her application for U.S. citizenship. Anna, in her usual way, had a new lie ready to explain each old falsehood. The FBI had already decided that her misstatements on the immigration and citizenship paperwork would not rise to the level that would allow for successful criminal prosecution. However, that did not stop Inspector Connelley from subtly insinuating that it was still possible. His goal was to convince William and

Anna that they should both remain in the United States while the investigation into Alice's disappearance continued. Inspector Connelley also told William that Anna, based on her recent press statements, might be considered both a hostile and material witness and that she might be extradited from whatever foreign country she might move to. William Parsons assured Connelley that he would see that Anna remained in the United States and that he would keep Connelley informed of his location when he traveled to California. William then informed Connelley that his trip to California with his sister Laura had been postponed for a week to ten days due to the illness of his sister's baby. He indicated that once the baby had recovered, Laura and he would depart for California. Once Inspector Connelley left the apartment, William Parsons told Anna Kupryanova that their planned move to British Columbia was off.

On October 1, 1937, at approximately 12:40 p.m., four FBI agents sat inside their surveillance location on Corporal Kennedy Street in Bayside. The agents had noted that Anna Kupryanova and Roy had just arrived in the apartment a short time ago. Suddenly, the microphone inside the apartment picked up the sound of William rushing through the door. The first words William uttered were, "Pack my things, I'm going now. I have to be there by two o'clock!" This was followed by a considerable amount of commotion, which included the sound of Anna sobbing loudly. Two of the agents immediately left the building and went to their government car. They located William's car in the front of the building and positioned themselves so that they could easily follow him when he left.

Ten minutes later, the agents spotted William running from the building carrying two suitcases. William was dressed in a gray suit and was wearing a brown felt fedora. As William was loading his suitcases into the car, Anna came out of the building and got into the front seat. William then got into the car and headed down the street at a high rate of speed. Followed by the agents, he drove directly to his brother John's home. When he got there, he raced into the house and came out again a few minutes later followed by Bunny Parsons. Bunny greeted Anna and then kissed William goodbye. William took off again and headed for the Triboro Bridge, where he crossed into Manhattan. He entered the Hudson Tunnel, which took him to Jersey City. He worked his way through the local streets and parked at a ship terminal. There William and Anna exited their car and headed for the ship berthed at Pier 9. It was 2:15 p.m. when they both boarded the SS *President Harrison*.

The trailing FBI agents quickly obtained a passenger list from the superintendent of the Pier 9 Dollar Line and ascertained that William

Parsons was one of thirty-five passengers on board and was sailing for Los Angeles. He would be occupying stateroom number 124. The records also indicated that William Parsons was sailing alone and that his car would be accompanying him on the voyage. The agents also determined that the *President Harrison* would be making stops in Cuba and Panama and would arrive in Los Angeles on October 17. At 3:00 p.m., the agents saw William and Anna leave the dock area together.

At 5:00 p.m., William Parsons returned to the *President Harrison* and boarded alone. There were no family or friends on the dock to see him off, and as the steamship pulled away from the pier, William could be seen walking its deck.

13

THE CALIFORNIA DEBACLE

It was clear by early October 1937 that the FBI's ruse regarding the Mary and Paul Jones letters had failed to produce the location of Alice Parsons's body. The only two investigative avenues that remained for Inspector Connelley were to continue the intense surveillance of William and Anna and to continue the ground search the areas in and around Stony Brook. For the continued surveillance of William and Anna to be successful, it was critical that the FBI stay one step ahead of them as they planned their move to California. Knowing William and Anna's destination and future residence in advance would allow the FBI to establish nearby surveillance positions and to insert listening devices within William and Anna's new temporary or permanent living quarters. Connelley was convinced that at some point, a recorded conversation between William and Anna would be captured and that captured conversation would lead him to the body of Alice Parsons.

The FBI's surveillance of William Parsons continued during his voyage from New Jersey to California. Although the FBI had not placed an agent on the SS *President Harrison*, it did arrange to receive copies of all cablegrams sent and received by William during his time on board the ship. These cablegrams included two cables sent to his brother John and one cable sent to his brother Oliver in Carpinteria, California. William also received two cablegrams from John Parsons and one from his sister Molly. The contents of the cablegrams were mostly related to greetings and travel arrangements. It was clear from the context of the cablegrams that William was expecting to join his brother Oliver in Carpinteria at some point in the near future.

The FBI's surveillance of Anna Kupryanova also continued as William made his way to California. In a letter to Director Hoover, Inspector Connelley indicated that Anna's bank account was being monitored and that the superintendent of her apartment building was on the lookout for any sign that Anna might be moving. In addition, the post office, Western Union Telegraph Company and Roy's school were all contacted and arrangements made to alert the FBI to any planned movement by Anna. Inspector Connelley also informed the FBI director that he had assigned Agents Meyer, Martin, McLaughlin and Ward to make a thorough and comprehensive search of the roads and terrain leading from the Parsons farm for the purpose of discovering the location where Alice Parsons was buried. In light of the weeklong search, conducted by hundreds of volunteers just four months prior, many within the FBI's hierarchy questioned this commitment of resources. This decision would soon become a problem for Inspector Connelley.

On October 18, 1937, at 9:15 a.m., William Parsons arrived at Pier 155 in Los Angeles, California, aboard the SS *President Harrison*. Waiting on Pier 155 in various surveillance positions were FBI agents E.F. Emrich, R.N. Pranke, F.M. Stone, R.P. Kramer and L. Whitson. William Parsons was immediately spotted on the top deck of the ship. While awaiting the discharge of the passengers, Agents Emrich and Pranke located the customs inspector at the dock and enlisted his cooperation. Inspector Meikle agreed to question William Parsons during the baggage inspection process as to his length of stay and his expected destination. Inspector Meikle was able to later report that it was William Parsons's intention to stay in California indefinitely and that his immediate plan was to stay with his brother Oliver W. Parsons at his farm in Carpinteria, California.

Agent Emrich boarded the SS *Harrison* and briefly spoke with its captain, Captain Ehman, on the ship's bridge. During this conversation, Agent Emrich spotted William Parsons on the ship's deck speaking to several persons who were later identified as reporters. When William left the ship, he was met by Alice's brother Howard McDonell and his wife, Jeane Marie. The three conversed for about ten minutes before the McDonells were seen leaving the area in their automobile.

William's vehicle was eventually unloaded from the ship, and he had his suitcases placed in the Dodge. He then stepped away from the vehicle and telephoned SAC J.H. Hanson of the FBI's Los Angeles field office as per his agreement with Inspector Connelley. During this call with SAC Hanson, William advised him that he had been interviewed and photographed by newspaper reporters at the time of his arrival at Los Angeles Harbor and that he was quite surprised that the reporters had obtained his arrival information. He also let SAC Hanson know that he would be staying with his brother Oliver in Carpinteria for an indefinite period of time. After completing this call, William returned to his automobile and drove away from the pier.

Trailing a short distance behind William's tan 1937 Dodge were two FBI surveillance vehicles. William made several stops, including a stop at a Western Union telegraph office where he sent telegrams regarding his arrival to both his brother John and sister Laura in New York. From there, he went directly to his brother's farm in Carpinteria, where he was met by his brother Oliver. By the end of that day, the ever-efficient FBI had secured coverage of all mail and telephone calls to and from Oliver Parsons's farm and had arranged to receive copies of any telegrams sent to or by anyone staying at Oliver Parsons's farm.

As William Parsons was arriving in California, Special Agent Martin and other agents were continuing their exhaustive search of the areas and roads in the vicinity of Stony Brook. This new search effort, which had begun in late September under the direction of Inspector Connelley, involved the examination of hundreds of miles of surrounding local roads and undeveloped lands. Then on October 20, 1937, in a totally unexpected and abrupt move, the FBI director ordered the search discontinued.

In a short but direct letter to the SAC in New York, Director Hoover ordered that the agents assigned to the search be immediately assigned to other duties. It was the first glimpse of what some would consider a faltering of the FBI's commitment to the continued investigation into Alice Parsons's disappearance.

The reason behind Director Hoover's order had all the appearances of an internal FBI power struggle. R.E. Vetterli, the new SAC of the New York FBI office, indicated that he wanted his agents removed from the Parsons case in order to conduct other investigations within the New York area. These would be investigations the he, Vetterli, would be held responsible for. R.E. Vetterli was a veteran FBI agent who had survived the infamous Kansas City Massacre just four years before. That thirty-second incident, masterminded by the notorious criminal Pretty Boy Floyd, killed three local law enforcement officers, an FBI agent and the federal prisoner they were transporting to Fort Leavenworth. R.E Vetterli and another FBI agent were seriously wounded in that machine gun attack.

With Connelley's attention now focused on a new kidnapping case in Chicago, some saw this as an opportunity to point out to Director Hoover what they believed to be the futility of Connelley's search plans. Inspector Connelley soon realized what was happening and reached out to the director via letter. On October 25, 1937, Inspector Connelley, in a carefully worded three-page letter to Director Hoover, adamantly opposed this action. He argued:

Dear Sir:

The investigation to date in this case indicates that the longest period of time that Anna Parsons could have been away from the Parsons home on June 9, 1937 after 8 A.M. would be the period between approximately 9:15 A.M. and 11:15 A.M. It has been rather definitely established that Anna can drive an automobile. The value of this later information is believed considerable by reason of the fact that Anna and William Parsons both have at all times tried to discourage the idea that Anna could drive an automobile, which they both persisted in since the date of the crime, June 9, 1937. It is reasonable to believe that Anna Parsons undoubtedly drove with the body, if this means of disposing of the same was used, not more than one hour's distance from the house at the time she disposed of it; that this travel was probably to the south or southeast, a territory with which she is thoroughly familiar.... The investigation to be made was a careful check of the roads leading from the Parsons home, particularly south and southeast from a distance as could have been reasonably covered by Anna Parsons on the day in question. A careful plan was worked out whereby they would check these roads and all roads leading off from such principal roads for a substantial distance on each side within the possibility of where she might proceed with the body in order to bury it. The hunting season may disclose some information as to this and also as the leaves fall it will make it much easier to detect the open places where digging could be accomplished in the wooded sections. As previously stated the finding of the body I believe presents a definite solution for the case and would be sufficient with the information we now have, to bring this to a very satisfactory conclusion.

I am writing at this time to verify that it was the intention of the Bureau to suspend all activity and search as above previously outlined. I had not instructed any further check in the immediate vicinity of the Parsons house as we have previously covered the grounds of the Parsons property very thoroughly.

Very truly yours,

E.J. Connelley
Inspector

Nine days later, Inspector Connelley received the following response from Director Hoover:

Dear Sir:

Reference is made to your letter of October 25, 1937, concerning the continuance of the search of the terrain for the body of Mrs. Alice McDonald Parsons.

This is to advise you that the Bureau intended and instructed that the search be discontinued.

Very truly yours,

John Edgar Hoover,
Director

As the surveillance of William Parsons in California continued and internal issues within the bureau continued to manifest, new evidence appeared that again directed a spotlight on the many lies told by Anna Kupryanova. This evidence arrived via the American consulate general in Calcutta, India. The consulate had finally located the reportedly dead husband of Anna Kupryanova, who she claimed was the father of her child, Roy. The consulate general had found Dr. Hans Raj Soni, who was now a professor of economics at the Benares Hindu University. On November 18, 1937, a sworn statement was obtained from Hans Soni in which he stated:

I went to England in 1918 and graduated from the Edinburgh (Scotland) University in 1920 and returned to India in 1922. Again left for England in 1923. In early 1926 I came across with Anna Kupryanova in London. She used to meet me at my place at West Kensington where I cohabited with her. Just before two weeks or so before the birth of a child we shifted to Kew Garden where she gave birth of a male child. I do not know who is responsible for this as she was a Russian Refugee and had been in liaison with a number of people. I lived with her till 1928 with a short break of about 6–7 months owing to some misunderstanding which arose between us. I returned to India in 1928 and joined the territorial staff of Hindu College at Delhi. I again left for England in 1930 and returned to India in 1931.

I cannot say how she was informed by the High Commissioner of India in London that I was killed in a motor accident in France. It may refer to any other Soni.

It is absolutely untrue that I had married the lady and if she possesses a marriage certificate in Brahmin language that must be a bogus one.

I do not know if the boy born to her at Kew Gardens in 1926 how christened in Greek Catholic faith and given the name Dionity or Rah Chandra.

I had never attempted to go to United States. I have not any passport for that country. I have got no connection with her at present. In 1930, on her request I had sent her some money as she begged for it as she desired to go to the United States.

On November 28, 1937, William Parsons was again on the move. He drove his Dodge to the La Playa Hotel in Carmel and told the clerk that he intended to stay at the hotel for two weeks. William was provided with the key to room 44. It was later learned that this hotel had been used by members of the Parsons family in the past. Hotel records showed that Molly Parsons had stayed at the hotel the previous year. During William's stay at the La Playa Hotel, he was in contact with the real estate firm of Del Monte Properties of Carmel. He told the Del Monte Properties representative that he was an artist and was interested in renting, with an option to buy, a place in the vicinity of Carmel or possibly Monterey. He was looking for a rental in a private location that had at least two bedrooms. He claimed to the representative that he needed the extra bedroom due to the fact that he expected friends to be occasionally visiting and staying overnight. It was the first clear indication that William Parsons was searching for a new home for himself, Anna Kupryanova and Roy.

The FBI surveillance team did not take up any rooms at the La Playa. Instead, they obtained rooms approximately five blocks away at the Pine Inn Hotel. They made arrangements with the La Playa manager to be contacted should William Parsons receive any telephone calls or leave the hotel. The La Playa also agreed to report any mail received at the hotel for William Parsons. In addition, agents obtained the cooperation of the local telegraph company and post office. The agents were now in a position to monitor all of William Parsons's communications and movements during his stay in Carmel.

As the surveillance of William Parsons continued in California, SAC Vetterli in New York was making additional moves to distance his field office from the Alice Parsons's investigation. In a November 29, 1937 letter to Director Hoover, Vetterli stated the following:

Dear Sir:

This office has in its possession a supply of lists of the currency prepared in connection with the above entitled case. These lists are dated June 10, 1937 and inasmuch as there was no occasion for the payment of the ransom, these lists were not utilized.

Unless otherwise instructed by the Bureau the lists in the office will be destroyed on December 10, 1937.

Very truly yours,

R.E. Vetterli
Special Agent in Charge

These currency lists that Vetterli wanted to destroy were part of the official record of an ongoing FBI investigation. It is doubtful that this handful of papers was causing an immediate record storage crisis within the FBI's New York office. To make matters worse, the man in charge of the Alice Parsons investigation, Inspector E.J. Connelley, was not copied on the letter. This action was simply indicative of the internal power struggle that was evident at the upper echelons of the bureau at that time.

William Parsons was keeping quite busy. In addition to looking at potential rental properties, he was busy communicating by telegram with Anna Kupryanova. On December 6, he wrote:

Anna F. Parsons:

Feel we together should have final talk with Levy and I also want to see some people about business property, so unless I hear from you to contrary tomorrow, will leave Wednesday, arriving New York Sunday. Will telegraph from Chicago exact time due in New York.

Bill

This was followed by another telegram the very next day which stated:

Anna F. Parsons:

Ben's telegram just came, and after thinking it over I agree would be mistake for me to make trip East. I will write full details of business proposition. See you soon.

Bill

Based on these communications, it seems that Ben Shiverts, Anna Kupryanova's attorney, recommended to William that he remain on the West Coast and not return to New York. This recommendation may have been partially due to the fact that the press was still focused on Alice Parsons's disappearance and the relationship between William and Anna. This was highlighted when the New York office of the FBI received a telephone call from Roy's school and was informed that one of Roy's classmates had brought in to the classroom a current newspaper article regarding the Parsons investigation. In the center of the article was a picture of the eleven-year-old Roy Parsons.

After just a little over a week at the La Playa Hotel, William Parsons was preparing for another move. On December 10, 1937, his room was changed from room 44 to room 38, due to falling plaster in his previous room caused by a three-day long rainstorm. During the move to his new room, William indicated to the hotel manager that he would be staying only three or four more days and then would be leaving for San Francisco.

On this same day, Inspector Connelley received a teletype at his temporary office in Chicago. It was from the FBI's New York office, and it indicated that Roy's school had been notified by Anna Kupryanova that Roy and his mother would be leaving for California on December 17 or 18. Anna wanted to obtain a record of Roy's school credits to take with her since they were not returning to Bayside. The FBI arranged with Assistant Principal Rockwell of Public School 130 in Bayside to draft the certificate of credits in such a way as to require Roy's new school to reach out to the principal for additional information. This, the FBI believed, would ensure its ability to locate Anna Kupryanova should immediate contact with her be lost. The letter given to Anna by the school stated:

42nd Avenue
Bayside
December 13, 1937

Roy Parsons was admitted to this school September 13, 1937, from Stony Brook, Long Island.
Official transcript will be furnished upon request.

Helen L. Baldwin,
Principal
P.S. #130
Queens, L.I.

In an effort to determine William's next move, FBI agents again approached the Western Union offices in both Carmel and Monterey. When they inquired as to any new incoming or outgoing telegrams for William Parsons, the agents were informed by both offices' managers that they had been instructed by their senior manager in San Francisco, M.T. Cook, that they were to provide no further information to the FBI until express authority was given by Western Union's headquarters in New York. This issue was quickly resolved the next day when Western Union's general counsel, F.R. Stark, sent a telegram to M.T. Cook authorizing full cooperation with the FBI. As this was occurring, the FBI's New York field office sent a teletype to the West Coast agents indicating that Anna Kupryanova and Roy were planning to leave New York for San Francisco by train on December 17. They were expected to arrive in San Francisco on December 21.

On the morning of December 14, Anna Kupryanova traveled to the Bank of the Manhattan Company in Bayside and closed her account. She withdrew the remaining $169 in cash and informed the bank officials that she was going to Florida for the winter.

On December 15, William Parsons suddenly checked out of the La Playa Hotel. He left instructions to have his mail forwarded to the Olympic Hotel in San Francisco up until December 18. After that date, the hotel employees were to hold his mail until he contacted them. Agents staying at the nearby Pine Hill Inn rushed to their vehicle and proceeded to a point about two miles north of Carmel. They concealed their surveillance vehicle in a small wooded area and took up a position that allowed them to observe all of the passing cars. Just a few minutes after their arrival, they saw William Parsons's tan Dodge heading in the direction of Monterey. William was alone in the car. With FBI agents following behind in their bureau Hudson, they continued a loose surveillance through Gilroy and San Jose and ended the mobile surveillance at the Olympic Hotel, located at 230 Eddy Street in San Francisco. The agents left their vehicle and proceeded on foot to the Olympic Hotel garage, where they immediately spotted William Parsons's Dodge. The time was 3:45 p.m.

One hour prior to William Parsons's arrival at the Olympic Hotel, the hotel manager Capp Balin brought FBI agents Trichak and Hammaak to room 521. All three agreed that this was the most suitable room for the planting of listening devices. Arrangements were also made for the agents to occupy the adjoining room 519 and to have all telephone calls to and from William Parsons's room also be accessible on the telephone in room 519. Other agents contacted the local telegram offices and post office in an effort to cover any and all forms of communication that might be used by William Parsons. Approximately one hour after William checked into the hotel, he left his room and asked where the closest Western Union office was located. He also requested directions to the St. Francis Hotel. Once William left the hotel, the hotel manager, Mr. Balin, used his master key to let Agent Trichak into William's room to test the quality of the reception of their listening devices. While in William's room, Agent Trichak noted an unfolded road map, a yellow cowhide suitcase, a pair of pajamas, a dilapidated brief case and what appeared to be a new black portable typewriter case. Once the audio check was complete, Agent Trichak and Balin left the room. An arrangement had been made to have the hotel's telephone operator, who had a good view of the lobby, jingle the bell on the agent's room phone when William Parsons returned to the hotel. However, the bell never rang that night; William Parsons did not return to the Olympic Hotel.

On that same day, Anna Kupryanova and Roy left their Bayside apartment at 8:40 a.m. and took the Long Island Rail Road train to Pennsylvania Station. She and Roy separated inside the station, with Anna then boarding a downtown subway train. The FBI surveillance team followed her first to her attorney Ben Shiverts's office and then to the Pennsylvania Railroad Consolidated Ticket Office on John Street. Once there, she purchased train tickets to California for herself and Roy. It was later learned that Anna Kupryanova refused to give her name to the ticket agent and insisted that the tickets be issued in the name of her attorney Benjamin Shiverts.

When Anna and Roy returned home that evening, she found a telegram waiting for her from William Parsons. The telegram stated:

> *Got here this afternoon and glad to get your letter and to know things are going nicely for you. Please send me a night letter Saturday from Chicago, Ill. Love to all, Bill*

The following day, December 16, 1937, another teletype was sent from the FBI's New York office to Director Hoover. It said the surveillance of Anna Kupryanova had produced firm information that she and Roy would be departing New York City's Pennsylvania Station at 11:35 p.m. on December 17. There would be a stopover in Chicago; they would switch trains and take the San Francisco Challenger to California. She and Roy were scheduled to arrive in San Francisco at 8:32 a.m. on December 21. The New York FBI office indicated in the teletype that it had passed on this information to the San Francisco office. A call was also placed to the acting Suffolk County District Attorney, John R. Vunk, to inform him of Anna Kupryanova's plan to leave New York.

The FBI's San Francisco field office was doing its best to stay on top of the Parsons investigation. Since William Parsons's arrival in California fifty-eight days prior, he had resided in three separate locations. Each place of residence required different forms of physical surveillance and constant monitoring of all incoming and outgoing mail and telegram activity. The San Francisco FBI office had now dedicated nine FBI agents to the Alice Parsons investigation. All nine of these agents conferred at their office on December 16. Each was shown photographs of William Parsons, Anna Kupryanova and her eleven-year-old son, Roy. The agents were then briefed by Special Agent J.E. Thorton about the purpose of the investigation. During the briefing, he indicated that it was their task to discreetly determine William Parsons's plans for a future residence in California, with a view of conducting microphone surveillance of his and Anna Kupryanova's activities and to maintain a complete log of all pertinent conversations.

The FBI's local resources in the San Francisco area were being tested at this time. Manpower resources were limited and became even more strained when, on December 16, Theodore Cole and Ralph Roe sawed their way through iron bars at the Alcatraz federal prison and jumped into San Francisco Bay. They immediately became Number 1 and Number 2 on the FBI's most wanted list, and the epicenter of the FBI search for these individuals was the city of San Francisco.

William Parsons returned to the Olympic Hotel at 9:10 a.m. on the morning of December 16. He ordered breakfast and had it sent to his room. Later in the day, he would have a conversation with the Olympic Hotel's assistant manager during which Parsons told the manager that he had lost fifty dollars the previous evening, intimating that he had been both drinking and gambling. William also indicated that he would be leaving the hotel on the following Monday, December 20, 1937.

The next day, William left his room at 11:45 a.m. He had scheduled a luncheon appointment with one of his former Yale classmates. Once William had left the hotel, the assistant manager unlocked the door to William's room so it could be searched by Agents Wine and Trichak.

In addition to the items previously noted on the day that William Parsons checked into his room, the agents found records concerning the probate of Alice Parsons's estate and personal letters from William's family members. There were no letters from Anna Kupryanova. The agents did find a Paragon Series notebook, which contained William Parsons' diary entries. The pages of the notebook were ruled, and the first two pages had been torn out. The entries began on June 9 and ended on September 4 of that year. Both agents worked quickly to record each date and diary entry onto separate paper. Agent Wine also obtained a specimen of the typewriting from Parsons' Royal portable typewriter that was in the room and then collected several sheets of blank paper from Parsons's Excelsior perforated writing pad. The agents also readjusted the microphones hidden in the room, including the one set up in the bathroom's ventilation grill.

Back in New York, in the early afternoon on December 17, two *Daily News* reporters parked their gray Oldsmobile in front of Anna Kupryanova's apartment on Corporal Kennedy Street and proceeded to her door. Anna spoke with the reporters for close to thirty minutes. Just as they were leaving the apartment building, a van from the Weissberger moving company arrived and backed right up to Anna's apartment. The two reporters returned to their car and repositioned themselves farther down the street so that they could observe what was happening. A short time after the furniture had been removed from the apartment and loaded onto the moving van, a black Dodge sedan arrived. The occupants of the sedan were John and Bunny Parsons. John and Bunny assisted Anna in loading her suitcases into the sedan, and at 4:30 p.m. they drove away. The gray Oldsmobile containing the two *Daily News* reporters followed them down the street.

Later that evening, Agents Murphy, Ward and Meyer established surveillance positions inside Pennsylvania Rail Road Station in Manhattan.

At 10:20 p.m., John Parsons, Bunny Parsons, Anna Kupryanova and Roy were seen entering the station. The group went down the stairway leading to the Golden Arrow train bound for Chicago. Six minutes later, John and Bunny Parsons exited the station. A check by the surveillance team of Anna's Pullman compartment showed that it was occupied and the shades had been drawn. The FBI began working quickly on locating the trunks that had accompanied Anna Kupryanova. The ticket check numbers were located, which revealed that the two trunks had a combined weight of 130 pounds. The FBI intended to examine the contents of these trunks before they were loaded into William Parsons's car in San Francisco.

Anna Kupryanova and her son arrived at the Union Depot in Chicago at 5:15 p.m. on December 18, 1937. Waiting for them at the Union Depot were FBI agents V.E. Smith, S.E. Dennis, John Sears and John Little. Agent Little watched from a distance on the platform as Anna and Roy got off the train. Anna and Roy proceeded to collect their luggage and transfer it to the Northwestern Station for the San Francisco Challenger train.

Once that was completed, Anna sent a telegram from the Western Union office in the train station. The telegram read:

> *W H Parsons*
> *230 Eddy Street*
> *San Francisco*
>
> *Arrived safely Chicago. Managed to change to lower berth. Everything all right. Roy is very happy and so am I.*
>
> */s/ Anna.*

The FBI agents continued to surveille Anna and her son until they boarded the San Francisco Challenger at 9:00 p.m. The agents watched the Challenger as it pulled out of the Union Depot station at 10:30 p.m. They immediately dispatched a teletype to the FBI's San Francisco office alerting them that Anna Kupryanova and her son had departed Chicago and were on their way to San Francisco.

On December 20, the surveillance team at the Olympic Hotel determined that William Parsons's current room would probably not be adequate for three people and that William might ask for a larger suite once Anna and Roy arrived. Working with the FBI, the hotel management planned to assign room 609 to William Parsons once Anna and Roy arrived. They also reserved the adjoining room 607 for the FBI surveillance team. In preparing for Anna's arrival, the FBI agents were confident that every effort had been made to ensure that any private conversation held at the hotel between William Parsons and the soon-to-arrive Anna Kupryanova would be clearly heard and recorded.

Similar arrangements were made at the St. Francis Hotel. Managers there were prepared to place William, Anna and Roy in a special suite with an adjoining room for the FBI surveillance team. However, the FBI still did not know where William intended to bring Anna and Roy once they arrived from New York. It was their hope that he would choose one of the three hotels that they were surveilling. Those included the La Playa, the Olympic and the St. Francis Hotel.

The evening before Anna Kupryanova's expected arrival, the SAC of the FBI's San Francisco office, N.J.L. Pieper, met with eleven of his agents. The purpose of the meeting was to establish a surveillance plan with the goal of determining William Parsons's and Anna Kupryanova's destination. Once that was established, every effort would be made to arrive at that destination before William and Anna and to install electronic listening devices in their living quarters. He informed the assembled agents that it was strongly believed by Director Hoover and Inspector E.J. Connelley that William and Anna's first private conversation, out of the earshot of Roy, would be both revealing and incriminating, potentially relating the location of Alice Parsons' body. This was reaffirmed later in the evening during a telephone conversation between SAC Pieper and Assistant Director Tamm. During that call, Tamm told Pieper, "The Bureau is particularly anxious, if at all possible, to establish a microphone surveillance covering the first few hours of conversation alone between W.H. and Anna Kupryanova after their meeting."

Two important events occurred on the morning of December 21.

First, the *New York Times* reported that Anna Kupryanova's attorney Benjamin Shiverts announced that William H. Parsons would be adopting Anna Kupryanova's son, Roy, and that Anna and her son were on their way to San Francisco to join William Parsons. The second important event occurred that morning at 6:20 a.m. That was when William Parsons checked out of the Olympic Hotel and did not leave a forwarding address.

William Parsons's sudden departure from the Olympic Hotel was not totally unexpected. Special Agent Louis D. Wine was monitoring the eavesdropping devices planted in William's room when at 5:45 a.m. he heard activity that indicated a possible move on the part of William. Agent Wine quickly left the surveillance room and moved a bureau surveillance vehicle about a half a block away from the hotel entrance. A short time later, the garage attendant brought Parsons's Dodge to the hotel entrance. William appeared and loaded his bags into the car. He left the hotel and was followed through San Francisco by Agent Wine. When Wine checked his rearview mirror, he saw that Agents Myerson and Geraghty had joined his mobile surveillance and were following behind him in a bureau Pontiac.

Approximately one hour before William Parsons checked out of the Olympic Hotel, FBI agent J.R. McCulloch and Special Officer Murray of the railroad police boarded the San Francisco Challenger at the Sacramento, California station. Agent McCulloch met with Conductor G.H. Payne and determined that Anna Kupryanova and her son were traveling in Section 2 of train car NZ. Officer Murray proceeded to the baggage car in an effort to locate their trunks. He later reported that the baggage compartment was full due to the heavy Christmas shipping and there was insufficient time to conduct a thorough search for Anna's trunks. Agent McCulloch remained on the train as it left the Sacramento station and placed himself in a seat that allowed him to monitor the comings and goings of the people in train car NZ. At 6:15 a.m., Anna Kupryanova and Roy appeared and headed for the dining car.

The surveillance team following William Parsons soon realized that there had been a change in what they had believed to be his destination. In addition, the surveillance teams monitoring Anna Kupryanova's movements also appeared to be somewhat confused about which station she would be exiting the train. Special Agent Charles Olson met the San Francisco Challenger at the University Avenue station at Berkeley. He immediately set up surveillance on car NZ as it pulled up to the platform. However, there was no sign of Anna Kupryanova or her son and the train pulled out of the station a few minutes later. Agent Olson quickly went to his car and raced the train in an attempt to beat it to its next scheduled stop. A short time later the San Francisco Challenger pulled into the 16th Street Station in Oakland. Agent McCulloch spotted Special Agent Olson just entering the platform and informed him that both Anna and Roy were still on the train but had showed no indication of alighting from the train at this station. The next and final stop on the line would be the Oakland Pier.

At 7:58 a.m. on December 21, 1937, Anna Kupryanova stepped off the San Francisco Challenger at the Oakland Pier and into the arms of William Parsons. William, Anna and Roy then proceeded to William's Dodge and loaded their hand-carried luggage. This all occurred under the watchful eyes of six FBI agents.

Special Agents Wine, Geraghty and Myerson were now detailed to conduct the mobile surveillance of William Parsons once he left the train station. The agents, using two separate vehicles, followed Parsons's Dodge through the city of Oakland using a time-tested mobile surveillance method known as the "Leap Frog." This involved repositioning the surveillance vehicles every few minutes so that Parsons would not see the same vehicle in his rearview mirror for any length of time. Parsons continued to drive south on Route 17 through San Leandro.

About one mile south of San Leandro, an incident occurred that would have a profound effect on the future investigation into the disappearance of Alice Parsons. As William Parsons traveled south down Route 17, he was being followed by Special Agent Wine at a distance of approximately six hundred yards. Suddenly, Parsons pulled his vehicle to the side of the road and stopped. Agent Wine, pretending to make no notice of Parsons or his vehicle, passed and continued down the highway. He made a left-hand turn at the next intersection. He traveled a short distance down that road and then made a U turn. He then positioned his vehicle so that he could see Parsons's vehicle when it went through the intersection. Agents Geraghty and Myerson had been trailing some distance behind Agent Wine's surveillance vehicle when they noticed Parsons's Dodge parked on the side of the road and watched as Agent Wine passed Parsons's stopped vehicle. Special Agent Myerson, who was at the wheel of the bureau car, had two options. He could either inconspicuously pass Parsons, as Agent Wine had done, or he could come to a stop. He chose to stop. This singular action effectively ended the investigation into the kidnapping and murder of Alice Parsons.

William Parsons remained in his car for several minutes. He then got out and proceeded down the road toward the agents' car. As Parsons approached the car on foot, Agent Myerson started his vehicle and was prepared to pull onto the road when Parsons stepped in front of the agent's vehicle.

As Agent Geraghty opened his car door, William Parsons asked, "What can I do for you gentlemen?"

Geraghty feigned ignorance and asked Parsons what he was talking about. Parsons asked, "What are you following me for?"

Geraghty made an indignant denial, which was followed by Parsons turning on his heel and proceeding back to his Dodge. With that, Myerson headed the bureau car down the road, passed Parsons's Dodge and continued south for approximately one mile. Within a minute, they saw Agent Wine driving toward them heading north. They tried to catch his attention; Agent Wine did not see them, however. Myerson pulled the bureau car behind a billboard and waited for Parsons's vehicle to appear on the highway. After a few minutes, the Dodge appeared and continued heading south.

Agents Myerson and Geraghty fully expected to see Agent Wine's vehicle tailing Parsons's car, but Wine's bureau car never appeared. Unbeknownst to Myerson and Geraghty, Agent Wine had decided to take another route in an attempt to intercept Parsons's vehicle thirty miles south in the city of San Jose. His plan to intercept Parsons failed, and when he called his office, he was instructed by SAC Pieper to return. Agents Myerson and Geraghty also called in to their office and received the same instructions; they were to immediately return to the San Francisco FBI office.

The decisions made this day by Special Agents Wine, Geraghty, Myerson and SAC Pieper had three immediate effects. First, the opportunity to immediately and electronically monitor William and Anna's first private conversations had been lost. Second, William Parsons and Anna Kupryanova, the FBI's chief suspects in the kidnapping and murder of Alice Parsons, were now roaming California out of both the sight and ears of the FBI. Third, the full ire of Director J. Edgar Hoover was about to fall upon SAC Pieper and the FBI's San Francisco field office.

Several hours later, William Parsons's Dodge was spotted in Salinas. The three-person surveillance team of Special Agents Olson, Johnson and Parry were now well aware of the incident that had occurred earlier in the day on Route 17 just south of San Leandro and were being extremely cautious in their efforts to keep Parsons within their sights and, at the same time, not be seen. Unfortunately, an overabundance of caution led them to lose sight of Parsons's vehicle again. This led to a systematic search of every street, garage and hotel in Salinas by the three agents. It appeared that William Parsons had again escaped the watchful eye of the FBI.

More than four hours later, the manager of the La Playa Hotel in Carmel notified the FBI that William Parsons had just appeared to pick up his mail. During a conversation with the hotel manager, Parsons mentioned that he would be staying at a place about two miles south of Carmel on Ocean Road and that he expected to be back at the La Playa to check on his mail sometime in the near future. In another unprecedented investigative error, the FBI failed to keep a single agent at the La Playa Hotel even though they knew that there was a possibility of Parsons returning to that location. They had also failed to monitor closely William's efforts to find a rental property with the Del Monte Properties Company. This failure would only compound the tide of anger that was quickly rising at FBI headquarters in Washington, D.C.

The three-person surveillance team of Special Agents Olson, Johnson and Parry left Salinas and raced to Carmel some twenty-three miles to their south. The agents arrived in Carmel at approximately 5:20 p.m. and continued their search through the streets of Carmel until 1:00 a.m. Practically every road, house and hotel in the vicinity of Carmel was checked, with negative results. The search was eventually stopped, and the agents agreed that Olson and Parry would continue the search in the morning. However, their first stop in the morning would be at the local utility company, Pacific Gas and Electric (PGE), to ascertain if any new accounts had been opened in the Carmel area under the name of William Parsons. It was also agreed that Agent Johnson would travel to Monterey in an effort to intercept Anna Kupryanova's trunks still in transit.

The next morning, Agent Johnson learned that Anna's trunks had arrived at the Railway Express Agency office in Carmel. As he was examining them, Agents Parry and Olson arrived and informed him that the PG&E records they had reviewed that morning indicated that a W.H. Parsons had applied, twelve days before, for the installation of service to be used at the Robin Hood Cottage, Lincoln Green Cottage Court, Carmel. They went on to say that it was a four-room cottage on Lincoln Cottage Court located just off of Carmel Road, approximately half a mile south of Carmel.

In another stunning investigative error, the FBI had failed to do a standard utility new account check for the Carmel area, even though there was every indication that this was the area that William Parsons had desired to live. There is no doubt that during the twelve-day period this information was available to the FBI, had they inquired, and there would have been ample time to install listening devices inside William and Anna's cottage and secure a nearby cottage as a physical surveillance post.

Director Hoover was very angry over the way the surveillance had been handled after Anna Kupryanova and Roy stepped off the San Francisco Challenger. Hoover went so far as to order Assistant Director Tamm to conduct a full inquiry into what had occurred. In a later letter of reprimand to the San Francisco SAC N.J.L. Pieper, Director Hoover wrote in part:

> *It is believed that two errors were made in the surveillance. I wanted to point out these two errors to your office in order that you would have the benefit of the Bureau's observations for your future guidance in handling similar matters. The Bureau feels that the first error was made when you, as the special agent in charge, instructed Special Agent Wine to return to the office. It was noted from the memoranda submitted that*

William, Anna and Roy's temporary new home at the Robin Hood Cottage, Lincoln Cottage Court, Carmel, California. *From the National Archives.*

when Mr. Parsons stopped his automobile, Agent Wine proceeded on by and thereafter called and informed you of what had occurred. Inasmuch as Agent Wine did not talk to Mr. Parsons and that there is no evidence that Parsons was aware of the Agent's identity or of the fact that he was maintaining a surveillance of him, it is believed you should have permitted Agent Wine to proceed to the vicinity of Carmel, California, where it was known Parsons and his party were proceeding, and there endeavor to again pick up the surveillance.

It is believed that the second error in the surveillance was made by Special Agents Geraghty and Myerson when they stopped at the same time that Parsons did. Naturally stopping when Parsons did would, to some extent at least, confirm Parsons' suspicions that a surveillance was being maintained. The proper action for the Agents to have taken in that case and in future instances, would be to continue past the car over which the surveillance was being maintained, in a casual manner, endeavoring to give the impression that they were not interested in their activities.

Very truly yours,

John Edgar Hoover
Director

Now that the opportunity to record William and Anna's first private conversations in California had been lost, interest in maintaining any form of electronic surveillance appeared to wane on the part of the FBI. In a teletype to Assistant Director Tamm on the evening of December 22, SAC Pieper stated in part: "Surveillance of present quarters extremely difficult. Doubtful whether any sound equipment could be set up even if surveillance was maintained from one of the other cottages. Instruct whether surveillance to be maintained."

This teletype was followed by a telephone call to Assistant Director Tamm the next morning, at which time SAC Pieper explained that it was his opinion that it would be impossible to maintain any type of surveillance without putting a male and female surveillance team, posing as husband and wife, into one of the adjoining cottages. He then argued that Parsons might move again, and their efforts could be wasted. It was during this telephone call that Assistant Director Tamm authorized the discontinuance of the physical and electronic surveillance of William Parsons and Anna Kupryanova, ending any chance of determining from them the location of Alice Parsons's body.

The FBI had made arrangements with William Parsons's real estate agent and the Robin Hood Cottage landlord to have the bureau alerted if William and Anna left their current residence. This finally occurred in the second week of January 1938, when Rae Welsh, William's former real estate agent, contacted the FBI's San Francisco office to let them know that Parsons had left the Robin Hood Cottage. A check at the Salinas Post Office indicated that William had opened up a new post office box in Salinas. The Salinas Post Office records indicated that William had secured Box 332 in his name, with a physical address "C/O the William F. Schmidt Ranch, Blanco, California." The "Schmidt ranch," as it was known locally, was located approximately five miles west of Salinas.

Special Agent Louis Wine, posing as a prospective property buyer, visited Postmaster Morton in the town of Blanco. The post office was a small one, run out of the general store owned by Mr. Morton. Morton was happy to speak about the area and all of its residents. During the conversation, Morton spoke about the Parsonses, who had recently moved into the ranch house across the street from his store. He explained that all of the land at the farm was under lease and was currently being worked by Filipino lettuce workers who resided in a bunkhouse near the ranch house. He said that although the Parsonses were living in the ranch house, they were not receiving their mail through his post office and they had not yet visited his store.

William later rented the Schmidt ranch house, which was located on the Schmidt lettuce farm in Blanco, California. *Courtesy of Three Village Historical Society.*

Agent Wine noted during his visit that the ranch house in which William, Anna and Roy were now living was quite secluded. He indicated that the ranch house was located directly north of Morton's general store and post office and could be readily identified, as it stood alone on a large plain with two enormous palm trees in front of the house. The closest neighboring ranch was approximately one-eighth of a mile away, and due to the surrounding open ground, it would be impossible for anyone to come near the house without being observed.

Agent Wine located and discreetly interviewed the real estate agent, Eloise Phegley, who had rented the Schmidt ranch house to Parsons. Phegley said that when she showed William Parsons the Schmidt ranch house a few weeks prior, although he indicated it was not what he was looking for, he decided to lease it for six months while he continued looking for a new home to buy. She said that she took Parsons, and the woman he introduced as his wife, to view the property. Phegley noted that the woman completely dominated William Parsons and was clearly the decision maker in the family. Phegley indicated that she had doubts as to their marital status, due to Mrs. Parsons refusing to sign her name, as was California custom, to the lease. The agent added that during one of their many conversations, William Parsons indicated that he planned on going into a grain brokerage partnership with a Robert Palmer and listed Mr. Palmer as a reference in his lease application. When Robert Palmer was contacted by Phegley, he told her that he hardly knew William Parsons.

Eloise Phegley mentioned one final oddity. The Schmidt ranch house had contained an operating telephone. William Parsons ordered it removed.

As William Parsons and Anna Kupryanova were searching for a new permanent home in California, Alice McDonell's family was busy trying to stop monies from Alice's estate from going to William. It was the family's desire to bring financial pressure to bear on both William and Anna by means of cutting off any sources of income from Alice's estate. To this end, Bess Williams, executor for the estate of Colonel T.S. Williams, suspended the disbursement of funds to the various beneficiaries under Colonel William's will.

Frank McDonell had visited the New York offices of the FBI on January 15, 17 and 30 and had informed the bureau that Bess Williams would be willing to foreclose on the unpaid $6,000 Long Meadow Farm mortgage if the FBI was of the opinion that such a financial move would assist the investigation in any way. William had recently sent a letter offering to pay half of his delinquent payments and half of the property taxes owed. Bess Williams rejected his offer. McDonell further stated that he believed that William was receiving financial support from his sisters Molly and Laura and from his brother John. Frank McDonell went on to state that in his recent contacts with the Parsons family he had found them all reluctant to speak about William and Anna. Inspector E.J. Connelley held the opinion that not enough was known about William Parsons's current financial position and that more information would be needed before he could offer an opinion regarding a foreclosure. To that end, Inspector Connelley requested that the FBI's San Francisco office conduct an inquiry into William's financial condition. The San Francisco office, which was still taking heavy internal criticism for the way it had mishandled the initial Parsons surveillance the previous month, issued the following response to Connelley's request:

> *The San Francisco Field Division will make appropriate discreet inquiries relative to the present activity of William H. Parsons and Anna Parsons in an effort to determine if any business enterprise is presently carried on*

by them or contemplated in the near future and will make further effort to ascertain the amount of their income and if presently carrying on any business. Will endeavor to ascertain the banks in which they have accounts and determine the sources of their income. Will make further effort to ascertain if Mrs. Laura Pratt or Molly Parsons are directly contributing to their support. Will generally maintain a surveillance in order to be apprised of their present whereabouts at all times and will continue the mail covers and conduct further inquiries as to business contacts and transactions as provided by the mail covers.

In early March, real estate agent Eloise Phegley was again contacted by Special Agent Wine. She reported that William was still looking for property to purchase. She noted that William appeared to be unemployed and that it was his custom to drive Roy to the Washington Grammar School every day. She commented that William had approached her recently and asked if he could take an option on the Schmidt ranch house for another year.

Phegley indicated that William had been paying his rent with checks drawn on a local account at the Monterey County Savings & Trust Company in Salinas. Agent Wine then interviewed A.P. Holm, manager of that Monterey County bank. Holm indicated that William Parsons had a balance of $576.61 in his account at the bank and that he had no other holdings with the bank. Holm stated that it was his understanding, after discussions with William Parsons, that Parsons was retired and maintained an income of approximately $150 per month. Holm went on further to say that he doubted William Parsons's financial responsibility and that the bank was not inclined to approve a loan of any kind for him.

On March 30, 1938, Director Hoover provided the first official word within the bureau that the FBI would be closing its case involving the disappearance of Alice Parsons. In a memorandum to Assistant Director Tamm, Director Hoover wrote:

While talking to Mr. Connelley he stated that the investigative possibilities of the Parsons case have been pretty well exhausted: that the only thing remaining is the finding of the body. I inquired if there was anything that we should turn over to the local authorities. Mr. Connelley stated that it might be well to call in Mr. Henry and give him everything that we have on the case and turn it over to him as a murder case; that they have a large personnel on the local force and if we turn those over to them they may institute a search and find the body. I stated that Mr. Connelley should do this; that if the body was found and the case brought to trial with witnesses would all be our men anyway and we would get the credit in the case. Mr. Connelley stated that he would do this in a few days.

Very truly yours,

John Edgar Hoover,
Director

The next day, Assistant Director Tamm responded to Director Hoover's memorandum, stating, in part, that it was his recommendation that the Bureau should:

Discontinue the assignment of any men to the case involving the disappearance of Mrs. Alice McDonell Parsons, the Long Island woman, and handle this case merely as a routine assignment. The solution of this case, it appears, could be effected if it were possible for Agents to devote their time to the investigation to the exclusion of all other investigative matters.

Respectfully,

E.A. Tamm

On April 20, 1938, Inspector E.J. Connelley wrote a lengthy letter to Director Hoover that outlined the inspector's conclusions and recommendations as it related to the Alice Parsons investigation. In that letter, he stated in part:

The facts in this case seem to be such as to warrant the conclusion that the victim in this case was undoubtedly disposed of by persons unknown to us, although the most likely suspects in this would be William H. Parsons, Jr. and Anna Kupryanova, which latter conclusion would be consistent with the circumstantial evidence available to us obtained as a result of our prior investigative activity.

He informed the director that he had reviewed the entire investigative file and was preparing materials to present to the Suffolk County District Attorney. He stated that it was his belief that the investigation should be left to the local authorities inasmuch as there apparently appeared to be only a violation of state laws and the FBI did not have sufficient personnel at that time to continue the investigation. He continued:

> *I believe this is the problem for the local authorities to make such a search as they believe desirable in an effort to locate the body of the victim or, they not being in accord with the idea in mind, they should make such other investigation as they care to make. It is believed that the body will be found within a radius of thirty miles from the home from which she disappeared on June 9, 1937.*

Inspector Connelley, still angry over the mishandled surveillance when Anna arrived in California, reminded the director of the consequences that had arisen due to the poor performance of the agents in the FBI's San Francisco office:

> *The original surveillance maintained upon Anna Kupryanova and William H. Parsons, when the former joined the latter in California several months ago having readily become apparent to William H. Parsons, Jr. as reflected in the reports covering such surveillance, and the house which he rented sometime prior to the time Anna Kupryanova contacted him there, not having been located until after the surveillance had been uncovered for suitable listening-in arrangements, it is believed that the possibilities of obtaining anything were frustrated and that in the future, we will obtain little, if any, information of this character. It is believed that if we could have had advantage of the first conversations of these two individuals when they got together upon the arrival of Anna Kupryanova in California, we might have obtained certain information along with lines previously obtained in the investigation wherein we had a listening device in the apartment covering their conversations, while living together here prior to the departure of William H. Parsons for California. Their reactions at this particular time, after a long separation, might have been of material value to us.*

Inspector Connelley's letter to Director Hoover appears to be the catalyst for what happened next. In an unprecedented move, Hoover decided to explore the possibility of legally removing Roy Parsons from the custody of William Parsons and Anna Kupryanova. The purpose of this dramatic action was to force William and/or Anna to reveal the location of Alice

Parsons's body. In an April 26 letter to SAC Pieper in San Francisco, Director Hoover wrote in part:

The Bureau desires that it be discreetly determined what action would be necessary under California Statutes in order to take the custody of Roy Parsons from Anna Kupryanova and William Parsons. The Bureau desires to know both the substantive matters which would have to be shown in order to establish them as unfit guardians for the child and likewise to know what procedure would be necessary in order to accomplish the same, providing that under California law there is any manner in which this can be accomplished. In obtaining this information, it is desired that there be no possibility of resultant publicity.

Very truly yours,

John Edgar Hoover,
Director

On May 5, 1938, SAC Pieper responded to Director Hoover's request via letter and reported that California law would not likely support such a removal action. Since neither William nor Anna had been charged with a crime, and any provable lewd and lascivious acts would have occurred in New York, it is unlikely that the petition for removal of Roy Parsons from the home would be successful. Pieper went on:

Courts are reluctant to separate a child from a natural guardian in the absence of strong grounds because of the possible shame and sense of being under reformatory restraint felt by a child as a ward of a Juvenile Court. The Courts consider the child's health (moral and physical) educational advantages and home life.

The mere fact that Anna Kupryanova lives with W.H. Parsons is consequently insufficient and the fact that she had illicit relations with Parsons in New York does not amount to acts in California.

N.J.L. Pieper
Special Agent in Charge

On the very same day that Director Hoover received the above letter, either by sheer coincidence or by an act of extreme intuitiveness, Anna

Kupryanova's lawyer Benjamin Shiverts released the following statement to the New York press on behalf of Anna and William: "It is not impossible that the friendship of Parsons and Anna Kupryanova might ripen to a point where an announcement of their intention to marry would be forthcoming."

This attempt on the part of J. Edgar Hoover at finding an avenue to force Anna Kupryanova into revealing the location of Alice Parsons's body appeared to have been abandoned, but it was not the FBI's last gambit. There were still more moves to come.

As Director Hoover was attempting to remove Roy Parsons from Anna Kupryanova's custody, Inspector E.J. Connelley was preparing to turn the investigative file over to the Suffolk County District Attorney's Office. Toward that end, on May 4, 1938, Inspector Connelley telephoned Assistant District Attorney Lindsay Henry and requested that he and District Attorney Munder come to the FBI's New York office the following day for a conference regarding the Alice Parsons investigation. Henry was told that the purpose of the meeting was to update and supply the DA with information that had been developed during the FBI's investigation into Alice Parsons' disappearance.

In what appeared to be a repeat of the previous year's lack of good judgment, someone within the Suffolk County District Attorney's Office immediately notified the press of the upcoming meeting. The morning of the meeting, the *Journal American* carried a front-page headline story of the supposed activities and discussions that were to occur that day at the FBI's New York office. On the morning of May 5, prior to the arrival of the Suffolk County District Attorney, the FBI's reception room was packed with reporters from every leading newspaper in the city of New York.

Present at the conference that morning were Inspector E.J. Connelley, Special Agent G.H. Meyer, Suffolk County District Attorney Fred J. Munder, Assistant District Attorney Lindsay Henry and the District Attorney's Chief Investigator John Hulsen. During the course of this meeting, Connelley provided hour-by-hour details as to what had occurred regarding Alice Parsons's disappearance on June 8 and June 9 of the previous year. He went on to brief all who were present regarding the bureau's surveillance activities at William Parsons's and Anna Kupryanova's Bayside address. This was followed by a briefing regarding their activities and current location in Salinas, California. This discussion included all information that was received over hidden microphones; William Parsons's signed and recanted statement concerning the chloroform; and the decoy letters from Mary. Inspector Connelley, with the previous day's press leak clearly on his mind, advised all of the Suffolk County representatives that none of the information that he had just provided had ever been released by the FBI, and if the information should become public, any resultant publicity would be their responsibility.

Inspector Connelley stated that any further investigation of this case would have to be done by local authorities. He made it clear that the FBI lacked the resources to continue in this investigation and that there was no federal violation apparently involved. Finally, he made it abundantly clear that the FBI would not be making any further investigations into this matter. He also made it clear that the Suffolk County District Attorney's Office would be supplied with any information it requested and would have access to the bureau's laboratory facilities if needed. District Attorney Munder appeared friendly and cooperative during the meeting and stated that he planned to institute a search by officers of the DA's office of the terrain in the vicinity of the Parsons home.

On May 10, just four days later, in another release to the press, District Attorney Munder stated that he had sent a letter to Inspector Connelley asking if the FBI had dropped out of the case involving the disappearance of Alice Parsons. Munder told the press that he had received no affidavits from the case: "None of my men have been assigned to work on the case. I must have all of the facts before I can proceed and I cannot say that any new material has been developed."

The one-sided press releases by District Attorney Munder continued. The *Daily News*, based on comments from Munder, even reported that the Department of Justice had refused to turn over any records of the Parsons investigation to District Attorney Munder. Inspector Connelley was, as he had been several times in the past, confused and frustrated with the conduct and comments by the Suffolk County District Attorney. The record of the May 5 meeting, as kept by Agent Meyer, clearly reflected the three main points of the meeting: the Suffolk County District Attorney had been briefed on every aspect of the investigation; any and all evidence would be turned over to the DA's office; and the FBI would not be continuing its investigation. These points, combined with the fact that District Attorney Munder had not raised a single objection during the meeting, led to complete bafflement on the part of Inspector Connelley about why the DA would suddenly claim ignorance of the very issues that were discussed and decided on at the May 5 meeting.

In a May 10 letter responding to District Attorney Munder, Inspector Connelley wrote, in part:

Mr. Fred J. Munder
District Attorney,
Suffolk County,
Riverhead, N.Y.

Dear Mr. Munder

…I assure you that I was astounded by the information that appeared in the newspapers on May 9, 1938.…We have not at any time indicated any change in our attitude, nor have we at any time refused you any information. In fact, any and all possible information available to us was furnished to you previously on May 6[5], 1938, as we believed in sufficient detail for all intents and purposes.

Under separate cover, as soon as same can be made ready for transmission, we are forwarding to you a report from our files containing all information which might be of evidentiary value now or in the future, together with suitable exhibits in this case. These will be rather voluminous.

Very truly yours,

E.J. Connelley,
Inspector

Inspector Connelley kept his word, and on May 18, 1938, a several-hundred-page detailed FBI investigative report regarding the disappearance of Alice Parsons was provided to District Attorney Munder. The report consisted of three main sections. Section A contained a summary report of all pertinent information concerning the disappearance of Alice Parsons. Section B consisted of various statements obtained from William Parsons and Anna Kupryanova together with pertinent microphone conversations and a written statement from William Parsons relative to his chloroform purchase. Section C consisted of a large number of exhibits, including the original ransom note, decoy letters and photographs of Alice Parsons's pin.

In a cover letter to District Attorney Munder included with the report, Connelley revealed a previously unknown fact. He wrote: "For your information, the entire investigation in the instant case was personally supervised by the Director of the Federal Bureau of Investigation, Mr. John Edgar Hoover."

The FBI report was delivered to District Attorney Munder by Special Agents Meyer and Whelan at Munder's private law office on New York Avenue in Huntington. A lengthy discussion was held regarding the file's contents, and Munder declined to take custody of the original ransom note. He asked that the FBI maintain custody until the note was needed in the future. A copy of the note was provided to District Attorney Munder the next day. Agents Meyer and Whelan insisted that District Attorney Munder sign a receipt for the file.

Agent Meyer noted in a later report regarding the meeting that it was apparent that District Attorney Munder had no definite plans for the further investigation of this case. Munder went so far as to acknowledge that the investigation conducted by the bureau was thorough and complete and that he was at a loss as to what further investigation might be conducted to move this case forward.

It was apparent to Agents Meyer and Whelan that District Attorney Munder was not eager to pursue this case any further. It was also clear to them that Munder did not wish to assume full responsibility for this case and seemed at a loss as to how to proceed. The bureau had already forwarded several recent crank letters to District Attorney Munder, and he seemed particularly annoyed with the idea that they were submitted to his attention for whatever further investigation he deemed advisable. It was apparent to both agents that District Attorney Munder was fearful and lacked confidence in assuming responsibility for the Parsons investigation.

Three days after the FBI provided the investigative file to District Attorney Munder, the bureau received word of a land purchase by William Parsons. The Del Monte Properties Company informed the FBI that a section of land just south of Carmel, in an area known as Hatton Fields, had recently been deeded to William Parsons. The physical address for the property was 3390 Mountain View Avenue, Carmel, California. It was here that William Parsons would build his new Spanish-style ranch house.

It had now been over a year since Alice Parsons's disappearance, and the McDonell family was showing its frustration with the lack of progress in the investigation. Members of Alice's family had made several attempts to meet with Director Hoover. On September 16, 1938, Frank McDonell appeared at the FBI's New York office. He reported that it was the family's intention to contest Alice Parsons's will and that they were contemplating appointing a temporary administrator for her estate. Frank wanted to ensure that the family's actions would not impact any current or future investigative strategies that the bureau might employ. Bess Williams had sent several letters to Director Hoover requesting a personal meeting. Even Howard McDonell reached out to Hoover from his Columbia Studios office in California and requested a meeting during one of Hoover's visits to Los Angeles. All efforts on the part of the McDonell family to meet personally with J. Edgar Hoover failed, and in most instances, they were politely reminded, in writing, that the bureau had closed its investigation and that all inquiries should be directed to Suffolk District Attorney Fredrick J. Munder.

Although the investigation had been officially closed, it was clear that Director Hoover and Inspector E.J. Connelley were still exploring new approaches that would lead to the satisfactory conclusion of the Alice Parsons investigation. One such move was cryptically referred to in a somewhat startling letter to Director Hoover from *Daily News* reporter Norma Abrams on April 4, 1939.

Norma Abrams wrote:

Dear Mr. Hoover:

After ten days submersion in legal records and Supreme Court rulings, the News legal department yesterday decided with the greatest of reluctance that it would be too dangerous to proceed with the plan in the Parsons case which I outlined to you.

Howard Carter went over the projected defense for The News very carefully with me, inasmuch as I felt strongly that it could be worked out successfully.

His final judgment was that without any proof of death, the News would probably become heavily liable in any actions that might be undertaken by Parsons or Miss Kupryanova.

However, neither Dick Clarke, the Sunday Editor, nor myself have entirely abandoned the idea, and we are hoping that somehow it may become feasible eventually in some way.

Thank you very much for your willingness to cooperate with me and The News. You may rest assured that the information you turned over to me will never be used in any other way. In fact, none of it have been discussed with any persons other that Howard Carter, nor will it be in the future.

Sincerely
Norma Abrams

Unfortunately, no further record exists about what Norma Abrams and the *Daily News* had actually proposed to J. Edgar Hoover. It is also unknown as to how many other efforts like this had been proposed or executed by the bureau after the investigation was turned over to District Attorney Munder. What is clear is that the FBI was more than willing to continue to collect information regarding William Parsons and Anna Kupryanova. One such collected record indicated that William and Anna were married on July 22, 1940, by a Superior Court judge in Hollister, San Benito County, California. There was also an indication that Roy Parsons had some years later graduated from Carmel High School and enlisted in the navy.

There is no official indication that the Suffolk County District Attorney's Office or any other local or state law enforcement authority in the state of New York continued any type of formal investigation after the FBI closed its case in May 1938.

The McDonell family kept true to their word and moved to challenge Alice Parsons's will in order to block any of the estimated $73,945 inheritance monies ($850,000 in 2019 dollars) that might have been due to William Parsons and his wife, Anna Kupryanova Parsons. On January 11, 1946, in order to avoid a lengthy and very public court battle, William and Anna agreed to renounce any inheritance that might have been due to them from Alice's estate. Alice's final will had been signed just weeks before her disappearance and had originally bequeathed $35,000 to her husband, William Parsons, and $10,000 to the housekeeper Anna Kupryanova. The final settlement did include a few pieces of Alice's inexpensive jewelry to be given to William Parsons and a $15,000 payment to Roy Dimitri Parsons that was to be held in trust until his thirtieth birthday. The remainder of her estate, which was originally derived from the estate of her uncle Colonel Timothy S. Williams, was divided equally among the children of her brothers, Frank and Howard McDonell.

On June 7, 1946, approximately six months after this settlement was reached, Alice W. Parsons was declared legally dead. The judgment was made by Suffolk County surrogate Richard W. Hawkins in a Riverhead, New York courtroom.

The declaration of Alice Parsons's death by no means ended what would be an intermittent but continued criminal investigation spanning an additional fifty years. It did, however, see the end of the Director Hoover's and Inspector Connelley's involvement in this case. Inspector Connelley and his agents' countless man hours of investigation, as documented by their nine-thousand-page investigative case file, led them to the conclusion that the persons responsible for the disappearance and death of Alice were her husband, William Parsons, and her housekeeper, Anna Kupryanova. William Parsons was a man who had clearly abandoned Alice much like her father had many years before, and Anna Kupryanova was nothing more than an intrepid liar who would say or do anything to protect herself and her son, Roy.

EPILOGUE

The question why William Parsons and Anna Kupryanova were never charged with the murder of Alice may forever go unanswered. Although the FBI clearly lacked a federal statute in this case, the local authorities could have easily placed the matter in front of a grand jury. The problem, as it usually is in cases such as these, presents itself as a level of proof. Having enough evidence to meet the probable cause threshold needed for a grand jury indictment is a far cry from the beyond a reasonable doubt standard required for a conviction at trial. The evidence in this case suggests that there may have been enough probable cause for an indictment, but perhaps not enough evidence for a conviction. When a prosecutor truly believes that a case cannot be won at trial, he or she may choose not to pursue the matter. This may be especially true when the prosecutor is an elected official and the case is one of a high profile. So it would appear that the question remaining is whether or not the evidence, lies and motives perpetrated by William and Anna were enough to obtain a criminal conviction for the murder of Alice Parsons in 1937.

When we look back at those who may have been responsible for the death of Alice, it is hard to perceive their innocence in light of the multitude of falsehoods that they told. The lies by both William Parsons and Anna Kupryanova were thoroughly documented by the FBI. Several of these lies pointed directly toward their guilt. One of the truly foundational lies, and perhaps the key to the entire case, had to do with William and Anna's claims that Alice had accompanied William to the St. James train station on the morning of her disappearance. It was confirmed that William did go into New York City on the morning of June 9, 1937. However, the fact that Alice accompanied William to the train station rests solely on the words of William, Anna and Roy. This lie was clearly exposed in a hidden microphone recording of a conversation between William and Anna in which Anna said, "You drove to the station in the morning." This was followed by William's reply, "That is what they say. But you know that isn't so."

An indication of guilt can also be seen when examining the issue of the missing half-full chloroform bottle spotted in the Parsonses kitchen on the night of Alice's disappearance. William and Anna's denial of its purchase, even its very existence, is inexplicable in light of the overwhelming evidence in the form of an eyewitness and sales records. This is compounded by Anna's own admission, again recorded by a hidden microphone, that she destroyed the very chloroform bottle she had denied ever having.

Adding to the likelihood of William and Anna's guilt is the original ransom note. It had been written on writing paper that contained the same watermark as paper found in Roy's room. It was paper that could only have been purchased at a Woolworth's store. This was further supported by Anna's own admission that she had purchased a different type of writing paper from Woolworth's in the recent past and bought her writing paper at the very Woolworth's counter where the ransom note paper would have been sold.

Then there were the circumstances surrounding the finding of the ransom note. The ransom note issue began with Anna's continual insistence that a search be made of the outside of the house and grounds for a possible note left behind by the kidnappers. It had been well documented that the Parsonses automobile had been twice carefully searched by experienced criminal investigators using powerful flashlights before the ransom note was found. A careful elimination of all those present at the farmhouse that evening would indicate that only William, Anna or Roy could have planted the note in the automobile after it had been searched.

Finally, there is the question of the author of the planted ransom note. Handwriting analysis by the FBI's technical laboratory ruled out both William and Roy as the possible author of the ransom note. However, the FBI's analyses of the dozens of handwriting exemplars obtained from Anna Kupryanova were deemed inconclusive. While Suffolk County authorities claimed that the handwriting expert firm of Osborne and Osborne had identified the ransom note's handwriting as belonging to Anna, no official report regarding that analysis exists within the records of the FBI or the records of the still-operative firm of Osborne and Osborne. Compounding this issue is the fact that all Suffolk County District Attorney's Office records regarding the Alice Parsons investigation were declared lost in 2019.

Another major lie throughout this investigation was William and Anna's denial of Anna's ability to drive an automobile and Anna's insistence that the family automobile had remained, unmoved, next to the house since the time Alice had returned from the train station that morning. As Inspector Connelley had surmised, in order for Anna to have disposed of Alice's body on the morning of June 9, 1937, she would have needed to drive Alice's automobile. It was the same conclusion reached by William and Anna when they jointly decided on creating the deception regarding her inability to drive. It was a deception that eventually failed when the trash collector Arthur Chadwick stated that the automobile had been parked in the separate garage on the morning of Alice's disappearance and later moved. This lie was further exposed when William's sister-in-law Bunny Parsons told the FBI that she had been present when Anna had taken her road test for her driver's license.

In addition to the lies, it is important to look back at the potential motives that may have driven William and Anna to murder Alice Parsons. There is little doubt that Anna Kupryanova was the driving force behind this heinous crime. William's motives may have been rooted in his unhappy marriage to Alice and his deep and never-ending need to please Anna. William had admitted to Inspector Connelley that he and Anna were involved in a long-term sexual relationship, and he told Connelley that he was wracked with jealousy whenever Anna spoke of other men's attention. William also admitted that Anna had dominated him and that he, in turn, had dominated Alice.

William had confessed to Inspector Connelley that he knew he had a problem with Alice and Anna that needed to be solved. He had even gone so far as to tell Anna that there had been one too many women in the house and that he would do something about the situation. William also admitted to his sister Laura Pratt that he was in love with Anna Kupryanova.

Anna's motives were always rooted in her need to protect her son, Roy. This started the year Roy was born and went on for many years, as she continued to tell falsehoods regarding the identity of Roy's father. This was followed by her continued assertions to William throughout the investigation that they needed, at all costs, to protect Roy. Finally, Anna succinctly summed up her motives in a 1961 statement to the Monterey Sherriff's Office during the continued investigation, when she stated that her marriage to William Parsons was more of a business arrangement in that she needed a home for herself and her son.

Finally, we come to the question of Roy Parsons's involvement in Alice's disappearance. First, the fact that Roy had not mentioned seeing Alice on his way to school in his initial interview suggests two possibilities. The first possibility is that the person conducting the interview was not thorough in his questioning. However, in this instance, the interviewer was Lieutenant Stacey Wilson, who gave every indication of being the consummate professional law enforcement officer. The other possibility is the fact that the eleven-year-old Roy Parsons may have been coached about what to say after his initial interview.

William had told Inspector Connelley that his arguments with Alice, regarding his and Anna's relationship, were frequent, loud and, at times, hours long. It is doubtful that any child living in such an environment could possibly be unaware of the discord. Yet Roy never mentioned any type of domestic disharmony during his numerous interviews with the local and federal authorities. What is clear is that Roy Parsons was very close to his mother and that Anna had the overwhelming ability to dominate those around her. It is important to remember that Roy was merely a child when Alice Parsons disappeared. He was a child who eventually grew into a fine young man who served his country and later became a husband and father.

William H. Parsons Jr. succumbed to a long illness on August 3, 1962. He died in his home on Mountain View Avenue in Carmel, California, at the age of seventy-four. His death certificate indicated that he was a salesman for the company of Parsons and Whitmore. The business was listed as a paper company. His present spouse's name was listed as Anna S. Parsons, housewife. A service was held at the Little Chapel by-the-Sea. His remains were cremated. Five months later, the deed to the home at 3390 Mountain View Avenue was changed and listed Anna Parsons and Roy D. Parsons as the owners.

Anna Parsons remained in the Mountain View Avenue home until 1971. Roy Parsons moved to Beverly Hills and became an accomplished artist, sculptor and gallery owner. Much of Roy's life can still be seen in the numerous coveted, museum-quality works of art that he created over the years. One such work of art is a color drawing of two robed female figures which immediately bring to mind the lives of Alice and Anna.

Roy and his wife, Allyn, eventually relocated to Dallas, Texas. After the sale of the Mountain View Avenue home, Anna Parsons moved to Guadalajara, Mexico. She was reportedly unhappy in Mexico and eventually joined Roy

William H. Parsons Jr. died approximately twenty-five years after the disappearance of this first wife, Alice Parsons. *From the archived files of the Suffolk County Police.*

and his wife in Dallas. Anna moved into a home at 550 Harvest Hill Road in Dallas and lived there until her death on February 1, 1982. Her death certificate listed her date of birth as February 17, 1900. That official record, like most of the official records that followed the life of Anna Kupryanova Parsons, was wrong. Anna S. Kupryanova was actually born on February 4,

1901. Roy Dimitri Parsons, the last surviving member of this tragedy, passed away on November 24, 2007, at the age of eighty-one in Dallas, Texas.

The never-ending investigation into Alice's disappearance was continued for forty years by Detective Sergeant William Stanton of the Suffolk County Police Department. His personal efforts led to several new, yet unsuccessful, searches for Alice Parsons's remains from the 1960s through the 1990s. However, there is no reason to believe that the investigation into Alice Parsons's disappearance is over. If the events of the past eight decades have shown us anything, they have shown us that there are always new questions and there will always be dedicated individuals, like the former Detective Sergeant William Stanton, who will continue searching for answers.

This chapter of this intriguing historic unsolved crime will now close with a final thought. The yearlong FBI investigation into the disappearance and murder of Alice Parsons brings to mind an old adage used to describe mismatched adversaries. That adage describes one adversary as playing chess, while the other adversary is playing checkers. In the case involving the disappearance and murder of Alice Parsons, both Inspector E.J. Connelley and Anna Kupryanova were playing chess—and Anna Kupryanova won.

Bibliography

Newspapers

Brooklyn Daily Eagle. "Rites Friday for Williams, Ex-B.R.T. Head." June 3, 1930, 3.

Chicago Tribune. "$25,000 Ready for Kidnaper to Free Wife." June 11, 1937, 4.

Daily News. June 13, 1937, 3C.

———. September 26, 1937, 87.

———. "Justice: The Mystery Remains." June 25, 1944, 47.

———. "Widow of B.R.T. Executive." November 26, 1936, 50. Alice W. Williams's obituary.

New York Times. "Col. T.S. Williams Dies Suddenly." June 4, 1930, 22.

———. June 13, 1937, 25.

———. "Colonel Williams' Estate to Family." June 17, 1930.

———. "Parsons Ransom Scouted by Bank." June 9, 1937, 8.

———. "Parsons to Adopt Boy." December 21, 1937, 20.

———. "Seeks Parsons Data." May 10, 1938, 16.

———. "Timothy S. Williams Better." August 11, 1926, 12.

———. "Vanished Heiress Is Declared Dead." June 8, 1946, 22.

Case Files and Collections

Alice C. Parsons Kidnapping Investigation. FBI Case File #7-HQ-1974, Investigative Files June 1937–September 1967, Box #14, Ransom Note recovered 6-10-37, Records of the Federal Bureau of Investigation, Record Group 65, National Archives II, College Park, MD.

———. FBI Case File #7-HQ-1974, Investigative Files June 1937–September 1967, Box #144, Memorandum from the Director, dated 6-10-37, Records of the Federal Bureau of Investigation, Record Group 65, National Archives II, College Park, MD

———. FBI Case File #7-HQ-1974, Investigative Files June 1937–September 1967, Box #144, Letter to the Director, dated 6-10-37, Records of the Federal Bureau of Investigation, Record Group 65, National Archives II, College Park, MD.

———. FBI Case File #7-HQ-1974, Investigative Files June 1937–September 1967, Box #144, Memorandum for Mr. Tamm, dated 6-11-37, Records of the Federal Bureau of Investigation, Record Group 65, National Archives II, College Park, MD

———. FBI Case File #7-HQ-1974, Investigative Files June 1937–September 1967, Box #144, Letter to FBI Director, dated 6-12-37, Records of the Federal Bureau of Investigation, Record Group 65, National Archives II, College Park, MD

———. FBI Case File #7-HQ-1974, Investigative Files June 1937–September 1967, Box #145, Memorandum for the Director, dated 6-12-37, Records of the Federal Bureau of Investigation, Record Group 65, National Archives II, College Park, MD.

———. FBI Case File #7-HQ-1974, Investigative Files June 1937–September 1967, Box# 144, Memorandum for the Director, dated 6-13-37, Records of the Federal Bureau of Investigation, Record Group 65, National Archives II, College Park, MD

———. FBI Case File #7-HQ-1974, Investigative Files June 1937–September 1967, Box #145, Memorandum for the Director, dated 6-14-37, Records of the Federal Bureau of Investigation, Record Group 65, National Archives II, College Park, MD

———. FBI Case File #7-HQ-1974, Investigative Files June 1937–September 1967, Box #144, Memorandum for the Director, dated 6-15-37, Records of the Federal Bureau of Investigation, Record Group 65, National Archives II, College Park, MD.

———. FBI Case File #7-HQ-1974, Investigative Files June 1937–September 1967, Box #145, Teletype to Director, dated 6-18-37, Records of FBI Case File #7-HQ-1974, Investigative Files June 1937–September 1967, Box #146, Investigative Activities Report 7-302, dated 7-23-37, Records of the Federal Bureau of Investigation, Record Group 65, National Archives II, College Park, MD.

————. FBI Case File #7-HQ-1974, Investigative Files June 1937–September 1967, Box #147, Teletype to the Director, dated 8-4-37, Records of the Federal Bureau of Investigation, Record Group 65, National Archives II, College Park, MD.

————. FBI Case File #7-HQ-1974, Investigative Files June 1937–September 1967, Box #147, Investigative Activities Report 7-302, dated 8-6-37, Records of the Federal Bureau of Investigation, Record Group 65, National Archives II, College Park, MD.

————. FBI Case File #7-HQ-1974, Investigative Files June 1937–September 1967, Box #147, Memorandum to the Director, dated 8-16-37, Records of the Federal Bureau of Investigation, Record Group 65, National Archives II, College Park, MD.

————. FBI Case File #7-HQ-1974, Investigative Files June 1937–September 1967, Box #147, Investigative Activities Report 7-302, dated 8-19-37, Records of the Federal Bureau of Investigation, Record Group 65, National Archives II, College Park, MD.

————. FBI Case File #7-HQ-1974, Investigative Files June 1937–September 1967, Box #147, Memorandum from the Director, dated 8-24-37, Records of the Federal Bureau of Investigation, Record Group 65, National Archives II, College Park, MD.

————. FBI Case File# 7-HQ-1974, Investigative Files June 1937–September 1967, Box #148, Certified Copy Birth Certificate, dated 9-4-37, Records of the Federal Bureau of Investigation, Record Group 65, National Archives II, College Park, MD.

————. FBI Case File #7-HQ-1974, Investigative Files June 1937–September 1967, Box #148, Letter from Robert Frazer, American Consul General, London, dated 9-4-37, Records of the Federal Bureau of Investigation, Record Group 65, National Archives II, College Park, MD.

————. FBI Case File #7-HQ-1974, Investigative Files June 1937–September 1967, Box #148, Investigative Activities Report 7-302, dated 9-22-37, Records of the Federal Bureau of Investigation, Record Group 65, National Archives II, College Park, MD.

————. FBI Case File #7-HQ-1974, Investigative Files June 1937–September 1967, Box #148, Memorandum from the Director, dated 9-22-37, Records of the Federal Bureau of Investigation, Record Group 65, National Archives II, College Park, MD.

————. FBI Case File #7-HQ-1974, Investigative Files June 1937–September 1967, Box# 148, Letter from Secretary of State, dated 9-27-

37, Records of the Federal Bureau of Investigation, Record Group 65, National Archives II, College Park, MD.

———. FBI Case File #7-HQ-1974, Investigative Files June 1937–September 1967, Box #148, Investigative Activities Report 7-302, dated 10-13-37, Records of the Federal Bureau of Investigation, Record Group 65, National Archives II, College Park, MD.

———. FBI Case File #7-HQ-1974, Investigative Files June 1937–September 1967, Box #148, Letter to Director Hoover, dated 10-14-37, Records of the Federal Bureau of Investigation, Record Group 65, National Archives II, College Park, MD.

———. FBI Case File #7-HQ-1974, Investigative Files June 1937–September 1967, Box #148, Investigative Activities Report 7-302, dated 10-15-37, Records of the Federal Bureau of Investigation, Record Group 65, National Archives II, College Park, MD.

———. FBI Case File #7-HQ-1974, Investigative Files June 1937–September 1967, Box #148, Report of Investigation, dated 10-19-37, Records of the Federal Bureau of Investigation, Record Group 65, National Archives II, College Park, MD.

———. FBI Case File #7-HQ-1974, Investigative Files June 1937–September 1967, Box #148, Letter to E.J. Connelley, dated 10-21-37, Records of the Federal Bureau of Investigation, Record Group 65, National Archives II, College Park, MD.

———. FBI Case File #7-HQ-1974, Investigative Files June 193–September 1967, Box #148, Letter from Director Hoover, dated 10-22-37, Records of the Federal Bureau of Investigation, Record Group 65, National Archives II, College Park, MD.

———. FBI Case File #7-HQ-1974, Investigative Files June 193–September 1967, Box #148, Letter from Inspector Connelley, dated 10-25-37, Records of the Federal Bureau of Investigation, Record Group 65, National Archives II, College Park, MD.

———. FBI Case File #7-HQ-1974, Investigative Files June 1937–September 1967, Box #148, Investigative Activities Report 7-302, dated 11-3-37, Records of the Federal Bureau of Investigation, Record Group 65, National Archives II, College Park, MD.

———. FBI Case File #7-HQ-1974, Investigative Files June 1937–September 1967, Box #148, Letter to Director Hoover, dated 11-29-37, Records of the Federal Bureau of Investigation, Record Group 65, National Archives II, College Park, MD.

———. FBI Case File #7-HQ-1974, Investigative Files June 1937–September 1967, Box #148, Report of Investigation, dated 12-10-37, Records of the Federal Bureau of Investigation, Record Group 65, National Archives II, College Park, MD.

———. FBI Case File #7-HQ-1974, Investigative Files June 1937–September 1967, Box #148, Teletype to E.J. Connelley, dated 12-10-37, Records of the Federal Bureau of Investigation, Record Group 65, National Archives II, College Park, MD.

———. FBI Case File #7-HQ-1974, Investigative Files June 1937–September 1967, Box #148, Teletype to FBI Director Hoover, dated 12-16-37, Records of the Federal Bureau of Investigation, Record Group 65, National Archives II, College Park, MD.

———. FBI Case Fil e#7-HQ-1974, Investigative Files June 1937–September 1967, Box #148, Investigative Activities Report 7-302, dated 12-17-37, Records of the Federal Bureau of Investigation, Record Group 65, National Archives II, College Park, MD.

the Federal Bureau of Investigation, Record Group 65, National Archives II, College Park, MD.

———. FBI Case File #7-HQ-1974, Investigative Files June 1937–September 1967, Box #145, Investigative Activities Report 7-302, dated 6-22-37, Records of the Federal Bureau of Investigation, Record Group 65, National Archives II, College Park, MD.

———. FBI Case File #7-HQ-1974, Investigative Files June 1937–September 1967, Box #145, Investigative Activities Report 7-302, dated 6-23-37, Records of the Federal Bureau of Investigation, Record Group 65, National Archives II, College Park, MD.

———. FBI Case File #7-HQ-1974, Investigative Files June 1937–September 1967, Box #145, Memo to Director, dated 6-25-37, Records of the Federal Bureau of Investigation, Record Group 65, National Archives II, College Park, MD.

———. FBI Case File #7-HQ-1974, Investigative Files June 1937–September 1967, Box# 145, Memorandum for the Director/Technical Laboratory, dated 6-25-37, Records of the Federal Bureau of Investigation, Record Group 65, National Archives II, College Park, MD.

———. FBI Case File #7-HQ-1974, Investigative Files June 1937–September 1967, Box #145, Investigative Activities Report 7-302, dated 6-29-37, Records of the Federal Bureau of Investigation, Record Group 65, National Archives II, College Park, MD.

————. FBI Case File #7-HQ-1974, Investigative Files June 1937–September 1967, Box #145, Memos from Director, dated 7-7-37, 7-8-37, Records of the Federal Bureau of Investigation, Record Group 65, National Archives II, College Park, MD.

————. FBI Case File #7-HQ-1974, Investigative Files June 1937–September 1967, Box #146, Investigative Activities Report 7-302, dated 7-8-37, Records of the Federal Bureau of Investigation, Record Group 65, National Archives II, College Park, MD.

————. FBI Case File #7-HQ-1974, Investigative Files June 1937–September 1967, Box #148, Investigative Activities Report 7-302, dated 7-22-37, Records of the Federal Bureau of Investigation, Record Group 65, National Archives II, College Park, MD.

————. FBI Case File #7-HQ-1974, Investigative Files June 1937–September 1967, Box #148, Report of Investigation, dated 12-23-37, Records of the Federal Bureau of Investigation, Record Group 65, National Archives II, College Park, MD.

————. FBI Case File #7-HQ-1974, Investigative Files June 1937–September 1967, Box #148, Report of Investigation, dated 1-15-38, Records of the Federal Bureau of Investigation, Record Group 65, National Archives II, College Park, MD.

————. FBI Case File #7-HQ-1974, Investigative Files June 1937–September 1967, Box #148, Report of Investigation, dated 1-22-38, Records of the Federal Bureau of Investigation, Record Group 65, National Archives II, College Park, MD.

————. FBI Case File #7-HQ-1974, Investigative Files June 1937–September 1967, Box #148, Report of Investigation, dated 1-25-38, Records of the Federal Bureau of Investigation, Record Group 65, National Archives II, College Park, MD.

————. FBI Case File #7-HQ-1974, Investigative Files June 1937–September 1967, Box #148, Case Summary Report 7-302, dated 2-12-38, Records of the Federal Bureau of Investigation, Record Group 65, National Archives II, College Park, MD.

————. FBI Case File #7-HQ-1974, Investigative Files June 1937–September 1967, Box #148, Memorandum from Director Hoover, dated 3-30-38, Records of the Federal Bureau of Investigation, Record Group 65, National Archives II, College Park, MD.

————. FBI Case File #7-HQ-1974, Investigative Files June 1937–September 1967, Box #148, Investigative Activities Report 7-302, dated 4-7-38, Records of the Federal Bureau of Investigation, Record Group 65, National Archives II, College Park, MD.

————. FBI Case File #7-HQ-1974, Investigative Files June 1937–September 1967, Box #148, Letter from Director Hoover, dated 4-8-38, Records of the Federal Bureau of Investigation, Record Group 65, National Archives II, College Park, MD.

————. FBI Case File #7-HQ-1974, Investigative Files June 1937–September 1967, Box #148, Letter to Director Hoover, dated 4-20-38, Records of the Federal Bureau of Investigation, Record Group 65, National Archives II, College Park, MD.

————. FBI Case File #7-HQ-1974, Investigative Files June 1937–September 1967, Box #148, Letter from Director Hoover, dated 4-26-38, Records of the Federal Bureau of Investigation, Record Group 65, National Archives II, College Park, MD.

————. FBI Case File #7-HQ-1974, Investigative Files June 1937–September 1967, Box #148, Letter to Director Hoover, dated 5-5-38, Records of the Federal Bureau of Investigation, Record Group 65, National Archives II, College Park, MD.

————. FBI Case File #7-HQ-1974, Investigative Files June 1937–September 1967, Box #148, Letter to Director Hoover, dated 5-6-38, Records of the Federal Bureau of Investigation, Record Group 65, National Archives II, College Park, MD.

————. FBI Case File #7-HQ-1974, Investigative Files June 1937–September 1967, Box #148, Letter to District Attorney Munder, dated 5-10-38, Records of the Federal Bureau of Investigation, Record Group 65, National Archives II, College Park, MD.

————. FBI Case File #7-HQ-1974, Investigative Files June 1937–September 1967, Box #148, Letter to District Attorney Munder, dated 5-18-38, Records of the Federal Bureau of Investigation, Record Group 65, National Archives II, College Park, MD.

————. FBI Case File #7-HQ-1974, Investigative Files June 1937–September 1967, Box #148, Letter to Director Hoover, dated 5-21-38, Records of the Federal Bureau of Investigation, Record Group 65, National Archives II, College Park, MD.

————. FBI Case File #7-HQ-1974, Investigative Files June 1937–September 1967, Box #148, Letter to Director Hoover, dated 4-4-39, Records of the Federal Bureau of Investigation, Record Group 65, National Archives II, College Park, MD.

————. 1961, SCPD CC#61-48752, Property Bureau Records, Suffolk County Police Department Headquarters, Yaphank, NY.

Timothy Shaler Williams Papers and Letters, 1836–1930. Manuscripts and Archives Division. New York Public Library.

About the Author

Steven C. Drielak is an internationally recognized expert in the area of Hot Zone Forensic Attribution. He received his master's degrees from John Jay College of Criminal Justice in New York City. He has over thirty years of law enforcement experience. Steven was responsible for the establishment of the Suffolk County Environmental Crime Unit in New York and commanded that unit for sixteen years. It was during this period that Steven participated in the cold case investigation of the Alice Parsons's kidnapping and assisted in two archaeological digs in the search for her remains. Steven also has served as a director within the EPA's Office of Criminal Enforcement, Forensics and Training in both the Homeland Security and Criminal Enforcement national programs. As the director of the EPA's National Criminal Enforcement Response Team he was responsible for deploying environmental forensic evidence collection teams to BP Alaska's Prudhoe Bay oil pipeline failures and the BP Deepwater Horizon disaster.

Steven has served as a senior forensic attribution instructor and program developer for the Department of Homeland Security's Federal Law Enforcement Training Center in Glynco, Georgia, and served for seventeen years as a National Academy instructor for the EPA's criminal enforcement program. He has also provided environmental forensic attribution training for the FBI's Hazardous Materials Response Unit. He has also provided international training to numerous countries within the European Union. He has authored and coauthored six textbooks in the areas of environmental crimes, weapons of mass destruction and forensic attribution. He has also authored two historical fiction novels. He has served as an appointed member of the International Association of Chiefs of Police Environmental Crimes Committee and served on the president's Interagency Microbial Forensics Advisory Board.

Visit us at
www.historypress.com